MW01617373

Strate

Second Edition

COLETTE TOACH

AMI BOOKSHOP

www.ami-bookshop.com

Strategies of War
Second Edition

ISBN-10: 1-62664-112-9
ISBN-13: 978-1-62664-112-9

Copyright © 2016 by Apostolic Movement International, LLC
All rights reserved
5663 Balboa Ave #416,
San Diego,
California 92111,
United States of America

1st Printing April 2016
2nd Edition July 2017

Published by **Apostolic Movement International, LLC**
E-mail Address: admin@ami-bookshop.com
Web Address: www.ami-bookshop.com

Unless specified, all Scripture references taken from the New King James Version®. Copyright © 1982 by Thomas Nelson. Used by permission. All rights reserved.

Contents

THE STAIN OF SIN – OVERCOMING CURSES

CHAPTER 01 — THE STAIN OF SIN — OVERCOMING CURSES

I would like to see a raise of hands of those that do not want to walk in the blessing of the Lord. When I say this, I know there is going to be silence. There is not one person that does not want to walk in God's abundant grace and blessing.

When I look at the Church today, I see so many striving to achieve the blessing of the Lord. They will go on fasts, pilgrimages, celebrate certain Jewish holidays, and subject their flesh to certain disciplines, all in the hope that they will obtain the favor of the Lord.

The reality is that although you know that you are saved and sanctified, you look at your experience, and it falls short. You know that you should walk in the blessing of the Lord as a believer, but you look at your life and think, "Why am I not walking in this blessing?"

The first memory that probably comes to you is of sitting at the dinner table with your mother saying to you, "No, you cannot have dessert because you did not finish your food."

So, you think, "I am not walking in the blessing of the Lord because I did not obey, perform, or do the thing that God told me to do. So now, God is withholding His blessing from me."

Then, you get into works of the flesh, and you search the Scriptures to try to find excuses of why God does not want to bless you. The truth is that you are looking at other believers who are walking in blessing, so you think, "Why am I not walking in blessing? What is wrong with me? Why am I not where God wants me to be?"

Your body gets sick, finances get stolen, loved ones die, and there is one bad thing after the next happening. Your eyes are on all of these problems, trying to seek a solution. This is the only reason why you should be open to dealing with curses in your life, because curses take your eyes off God.

God's Blessing is Your Inheritance

I am cutting to the chase right now, and I am making a statement here. God is not withholding His blessing from you. As a born-again child of God, His blessing is your inheritance.

The storehouses of heaven belong to you. You own the key. You are ruling and reigning with Christ. So, if you are not experiencing that blessing, it is not God that is withholding it, but rather a work of the enemy that is blocking it.

By the end of this chapter, not only will you understand this blockage, but you will also have the power in your hands to remove it. Curses take away our faith in God, and this is why we have to deal with them.

Can we still walk in the blessing of the Lord without dealing with curses? Absolutely! You can still walk in the abundant blessing of the Lord without doing spiritual warfare because faith can move mountains.

If you have enough faith, you could skip this message completely because it would not matter if Lucifer himself were coming against you. However, when problems or curses manifest in your life, they take your eyes off Christ.

Curses take your heart off faith and corrode your hope, and your love. Sure, we can overcome by pure willpower and by standing in faith. I am sure that the many times you have had success in your life, it is when you put your eyes on Christ and overcame with faith.

REMOVING YOUR FAITH BLOCKERS

Yet, why not make it easier on yourself and get rid of the things that are a hindrance to your faith so that it is so much easier to believe God? Imagine for a moment that you have been walking in pure faith, without doing warfare, and you have been getting results.

Now, imagine that you have removed the faith blockers and the love blockers in your life, and then you exercise the same portion of faith to your circumstances. What do you think is going to happen?

You will have an explosion take place in your life. That is what this subject is about. It is about removing the hindrances to your faith. It is about taking away those things that destroy the fruit of the spirit that is in you.

We are human. When I feel sick, I am grumpy... just ask any of my family. The Lord knows I should be walking in the fruit of the spirit, but I still feel like biting your head off because you just woke me up.

I could still, by sheer willpower, walk in the spirit, but it would make it so much easier for me to be a nice person to be around if I was not sick. So then, let's just get rid of sickness. Let's get rid of the curse of theft, destruction, or poverty, and all the works of the enemy in your life, so that the mustard seed of faith that you have can flourish and abound without restriction.

BUILDING CITY WALLS

When the Lord started teaching me the subject of curses afresh, He showed me a city. The city had a beautiful wall built all around it, just like in the day of Ezra and Nehemiah when they built that wall for protection.

The Lord said to me, "My child, this is my shield of protection around you. The Holy Spirit encamps around you, and you have a wall of protection." Then, I saw something happening as I was watching as a watchman on the wall.

I saw all these arrows coming at the wall from without. I saw javelins, arrows, and other weapons of warfare coming to smash against the walls to try to shake and break them - but they could not. The walls stood fast.

Then, I saw another picture. I saw that there was a crack in the wall. When I looked down, I saw that there was a small hole at the base of the wall of my city. I saw how easily the enemy crept under that wall to bring attack.

The Lord said to me, "That picture that I have just shown you is a picture of how curses work in your life. You are a city set upon a hill. I am there for your protection, but there is a crack in your wall."

CURSES VS. SPIRITUAL WARFARE

You can keep on fighting the enemy as he continues to steal, kill, and destroy... or you can just patch up your wall so that he cannot get in anymore. By the end of this chapter, I would have explained to you the difference between curses and spiritual warfare.

This particular chapter is not about spiritual warfare, but about curses. I will get into spiritual warfare further down. Right now, we are going to take a look at the holes in your wall. You do not need to fear curses, sickness, poverty, theft or any work of the enemy ever again. You can be free.

IDENTIFYING THE HOLES IN YOUR WALL

The first thing that you need to know is your position in Christ.

John 5:22 says,

> *For the Father judges no one, but has*
> *committed all judgment to the Son*

Hebrews 12:9-10 says,

> *Furthermore, we have had human fathers who*
> *corrected us, and we paid them respect. Shall*
> *we not much more readily be in subjection to the*
> *Father of spirits and live?*
> *10 For they indeed for a few days chastened us*
> *as seemed best to them, but He for our profit,*
> *that we may be partakers of His holiness.*

Something changed in the dynamic between God and man when Christ died on the cross for you. In the Old Testament, we see a God of judgment. He is indeed a God to be feared and who judged and punished the sin of His people.

He killed them, smote them, and wiped them out. He sent them off into a foreign land, and He brought them into captivity. He tore them down. This is the consuming fire of the Father.

However, along came Jesus who was sinless - perfect. He was so perfect that the judgment of the Father was committed to Him.

In other words, the Father said to Jesus, "Not only does your blood atone for the sins of the people that believe in you, but the judgment is yours and no longer mine. I will no longer judge my people. Jesus, it is for you to judge your people."

Do you know what Jesus said? He said, "I did not come to judge this world, but to save it." We are free from the punishment of sin given by the Father. Let that sink in for a minute.

I want to share an illustration that my dad always shared when He spoke about our position in Christ.

You sin a terrible sin, and the Father says, "You sinned. You must be punished."

Then, Jesus raises His hand and says, "Look Father, that sin is paid for." He appeals at the right hand of the Father.

Even better, you are covered by the blood of Jesus Christ. So when the Father looks at you, do you know what He sees?

Do you think He sees your sin? No, He sees the blood of Christ that has washed away the sin. When the Father looks at you now, He sees righteousness.

THE NEW TESTAMENT REVOLUTION

The relationship changed between the Old and New Testament. In the Old Testament, He was a God of judgment. In the New Testament, according to Hebrews 12:9, He became our Abba, Father.

I looked up many words like punish and judgment in the Scriptures to find out if God still punishes His children for their sin in the New Testament. I could not find one. However, I did find many that said that He chastises, or disciplines, you as a father disciplines his child.

He is not disciplining you because you sinned, and He wants to make you pay, but so that you can get it right next time. Why do I punish my children? If I am a good mother, I am doing it so that my children can be a success and learn to discipline themselves one day.

That is our relationship with the Father. God is not the author of curses in the New Testament. If you are a blood-bought child of God, you do not need to fear the curse of the Father any longer.

JESUS TORE THE VEIL

He whom the Son sets free is free indeed. When Jesus hung on that cross and cried out, "It is finished," He did not mean that it was halfway done. He said that it was finished. Then, the temple shook, the curtain was torn, and the Holy of Holies was made accessible.

Why could we go into the Holy of Holies all of a sudden? We could go into the Holy of Holies because sin was no longer on us. His blood now covered our sin. Before then, no one could go into the Holy of Holies without a blood sacrifice, or else they would die because God could not be with sinful man.

Yet, it has changed. Does that make you sinless? No, not at all, but it does make you free from the judgment of God. It gives you a position of favor in Him. He corrects you for your own good.

You do not need to fear His punishment for your sins. Why are you having a hard time then? Why are you seeing all of these things that appear to be punishment for your sin? Why are you battling? That is the point of this chapter, right? I am getting there. Give me a moment. I am on my soapbox right now.

So, is the judgment of God completely eradicated in the New Testament? No, it is not. It is only eradicated for the saved, but His judgment remains to the world.

GOD'S JUDGMENT TO THE WORLD REMAINS

The judgment of God remains for those who are not washed by the blood of Christ. In fact, just try to mess with His Church. Go to the book of Revelation and do some reading there sometime.

You will read about the curses on those that came against the Church. Also, read the book of Jude and see what happens to those that are unjust and try to come against the Church.

> *1 Corinthians 5:13 But those who are outside God judges. Therefore put away from yourselves the evil person.*

It says that God will judge the unjust and the sinner, the one who is not born again and not redeemed by the blood. Judgment remains for the world. God continues to judge the unbeliever, but He no longer judges the believer.

The blood of Christ covers us from that judgment, but you are forgetting something important.

Ephesians 1:7 says,

> *In Him we have redemption through His blood, the forgiveness of sins, according to the riches of His grace*

Ephesians 4:26-27 says,

> *Be angry, and do not sin": do not let the sun go down on your wrath,*
> *27 nor give place to the devil*

Herein lies the secret - the answer that you have been looking for. God is not judging you, but there is one who is. His name is satan, the accuser of the brethren. He is the one who is wearing down the saints and looking for any opportunity that he can possibly find to come and steal, kill, and destroy.

God does not judge you for your sin, but your sin makes a hole in the wall of the city, allowing the enemy to gain access to your life. Can you see what a dramatic shift between the Old and the New Testament this is?

Satan Comes to Tempt You

In the New Testament, satan is the author of curses. He is the one stealing, killing, and destroying. You do not have to fear the judgment of the Lord for disobeying His laws, but if you do not walk in the spirit, there is one out there who is only too happy to take back the land.

When Adam and Eve were in the Garden of Eden, satan tempted Eve to sin. What happened when she sinned? She opened a whole door in their wall, and because the blood of Christ was not there to cover them, they opened themselves wide to the judgment of the Lord because they walked in disobedience.

Yet, we have the blood of Christ, so why do we have these curses? We have these curses because we have an enemy that will use every opportunity that he can to destroy us. Let me tell you something, if you do not put that sin under the blood, satan will most certainly take full advantage of it.

The Sin Subject

Think about it. As I was reading up on this subject, I was amazed at how often we are told to ask forgiveness of our sins in the New Testament. The Lord said to me that people make two great mistakes in His body when it comes to this subject.

On one hand, they think that He is punishing them left, right, and center for their sins. So, they quickly repent of every sin that they can think of, because they are afraid that He is going to punish them.

However, they never really have a true heart of repentance. They are always just dealing with their "flesh sins." They think that they will lose their salvation every five minutes and that the Lord is going to smite them and kick them out of His family, because they had a bad night and sinned.

So, they walk around in fear of the Lord. Satan is only too happy to take a ride on that fear, because that fear separates you from the love of God. Your heart becomes condemned, and you cannot approach the throne of grace, and satan laughs all the way to the bank. (Hebrews 4:16)

Then, the Lord said to me that the other half of the body of Christ is on the "grace chariot," which is the side that I grew up on. The grace side says, "We have been forgiven once and for all. So, why do I need to continually repent of my sins when the blood of Christ continually covers me?"

YOUR POSITION VERSUS YOUR EXPERIENCE IN CHRIST

When you think like this, you are mistaking your position with your experience in Christ. Yes, your position in Christ is when the Father looks at you and sees you as free, sinless, and pure. Sin has indeed been washed away in His sight.

However, you have an enemy, and he is not going to turn a blind eye to every hook, line, and sinker that you give him. If that sin has not been deliberately placed under the blood, you are free game. It is satan's ace card.

James 4:7 says that we are to submit ourselves to the Lord and resist the devil, and then he will flee from us.

"I am born again. Therefore, I am submitted to the Lord, right?"

Well, maybe yesterday you were submitted to the Lord, but maybe not today, because there were a few things that you did yesterday that you need to submit to the blood of Christ. You need to put that sin under the blanket of Jesus' blood.

You are not doing this so that the Father does not judge you, because the Father does not see the sin anyway. You need to put the sin under the blood so that the devil cannot use it as a weapon against you.

Do you understand that? It is a powerful revelation. We are to submit our sins to the Lord and ask for forgiveness for our sins to keep our hearts pure. Why do you think Paul was going on and on about walking in the spirit?

He knew that when we walk in the flesh, we walk in sin. I asked the Lord to give me a picture of what curses really look like because I wanted to understand it more. He took me to Deuteronomy 28.

CHAPTER 02

LIST OF CURSES

CHAPTER 02 – LIST OF CURSES

I am going to go through a list of curses that can be manifested in your life because of sin. I have summarized it to twenty curses. Go through this list with me and take a look at your own life.

If you have any of these manifestations in your own life, then there is an open door that satan is using to destroy you. God is not trying to get you down or destroy you. Satan is stealing that blessing from you.

So, let's weed him out. Go over to your wall, find every hole, and seal it up. Here are the signs:

1. Financial struggles (basket and store)
2. Poverty
3. Continual sickness (fruit of your body)
4. Unsuccessful - Everything you try to work at fails
5. Rain/blessing always held back (promises never fulfilled)
6. Enemies overcome you
7. Disfavor
8. Adultery – loss in relationships (marry a wife and another will have her)
9. Will never eat the fruit of your labor (build a house - another lives in it)
10. Theft (possessions taken away)
11. Pain and suffering
12. Work hard and reap little

13. Invest into others, but they will leave you and follow others (ministry)
14. The world given promotion – you are demoted
15. Always in debt (always borrowing, never the lender)
16. Destruction - continual attack against your possessions
17. You will "eat up" and lose the good things God has given you
18. Unrest – no peace to settle. Always striving
19. Strife
20. Fear

Now, this is the summarized list. However, the good news is that Jesus came to set us free from the curse of the law. We no longer have to suffer with these things, but we do need to deal with them, and that means dealing with our flesh.

TIME TO DEAL WITH YOUR SIN

Dealing with your flesh means that you will have to deal with your sin - that nasty three-letter word that no one wants to preach about anymore. Everyone wants to be nice and phlegmatic and say, "I understand. Let's go sit on the psychologist's couch so that we can see why your mother treated you the way that she did, so that you can excuse your sin."

If that is the way that you want to do it, then go for it. However, I do not know about you, but whatever it takes to break free of these curses in my life, even if it means dealing with my sin and flesh and learning to walk in the spirit - I am going to do it!

If it means that I have to admit to pride and every other sin so that I can break free, and my children after me can break free, then I am going to do it!

I am reminded of a family that heard our curses teaching and got very excited about it. They discovered that they had a lot of generational curses and things that they had received from their parents, so they went through their entire house and got rid of anything that could have been a "contamination."

They prayed differently, they fasted, they got rid of all their furniture, and before long, they were barely sleeping on mattresses because they did not want to have any generational curses.

They broke links with their family and did all kinds of crazy things. However, they never did this one little thing. They never dealt with their sin, pride, and their spirit of rebellion.

WORKS ARE DEAD

I see this all the time in the church. You fast, pray, go on holidays, feasts, celebrations, and pay all these prices. You travel to different countries, do warfare, and you are even prepared to be a martyr... but you do not want to deal with your sin.

You do not want to admit that you are bitter or full of pride. You are doing all these things and performing this big song and dance, hoping that God will bless you. God has already blessed you with every spiritual blessing in heavenly places with Christ (Ephesians 1:7).

He has already blessed you with every blessing that you can imagine. God is not the problem here. The devil is the problem. He is the one blocking the blessing. However, when you give him license and play on his playground, then James 1:15 happens.

James 1:15 says,

> *Then, when desire has conceived, it gives birth to sin; and sin, when it is full- grown, brings forth death.*

Here is the fruit of your curse. This is why you are walking in those curses in your life. Sin is the root of every curse that is manifest in your life. When you submit yourself to sin, it becomes your master.

The Scriptures say that whomever you submit your body to becomes your master. When you do that, you enter satan's playing field. You step out of the covering of the blood that God gave you, and you give satan license in your life.

He is a champ on his playing field, and he will take you out. God does not need to judge us for our sins, because we judge ourselves. We are responsible to bring that sin under the blood so that it can be washed away, and satan does not have access to our lives.

The Word of God tells you to walk in the spirit, but sometimes, you have a bad day and walk in the flesh. We all do it. It is not like you walk in the spirit twenty-four hours a day. There are some days that I feel that I am the biggest heathen on the earth.

I know that Paul had many of these days. He said, "Oh wretched man that I am. Who will deliver me?" We all have those days.

WALKING IN THE FLESH PRODUCES SIN

So, we do this bounce between walking in the spirit and walking in the flesh. Is walking in the flesh sin? That is a tricky question because walking in the flesh is not a sin in itself, but it is more accurate to say that walking in the flesh produces sin.

When you walk in the spirit, the Word says that you produce the fruits of the spirit, right? So then, when you walk in the flesh, you are going to start experiencing the works of the flesh.

Sin does not immediately jump up and bite you on the butt. It does not work that way. You start walking in the flesh, and by doing that, you start sowing a little seed. Then, you walk more and more in the flesh and next thing you know, there is a bit of anger, frustration, and jealousy there.

Then, that little seed starts to mature and grow. The more you sin, the more you nurture that tree, and that tree ends up producing fruit. Then, you start eating of that tree. When that happens, you have a full-blown curse manifesting in your life.

You need to chop down that tree. The Scriptures say that you need to lay the axe to the root of the tree to tear it down. However, the starting point of any "flesh tree" is that you get out of the spirit, and you start walking in the flesh.

Then, you allow that flesh to start becoming sin, and satan is only too glad to help fertilize that tree, breathe on it, trim it, and make sure that it flourishes nicely. As long as he has that tree in your life, he can use it as an access point to your city any time that he pleases.

The thing that you need to understand about a curse is that it is not the fruit of a once-off sin.

This was a revelation that really encouraged me. When you see these curses manifesting in your life, it is not just because you swore at the driver on your way to work or because you had a fight with your wife.

FROM SEED, TO TREE, TO FRUIT

If you commit just one sin, then that is just sin that you can put under the blood. I am talking about continual sin that has not been repented of, and that has gone from seed, to tree, to fruit.

Once that fruit has matured on the tree, the fruit becomes a curse. This is produced by walking in the flesh, remaining in the flesh, and continuing to walk in the same sin again and again. If you want to see some of the sins, you can see them in Galatians 5.

I will share them with you here. These are just some of the sins that will start manifesting in your life. The Word mentions many sins, but this is just a good stab of conviction here.

Adultery, illicit sex, moral impurities, unbridled lust, serving false gods, sorcery, hatred, strife, jealousy, explosive anger, self-promotion, division, envy, murder, and drunkenness.

If you got drunk once because you went to a wedding and had too much wine, is God going to slay you? No. God does not judge believers, remember? Yet, I would repent on the way home.

However, if you keep doing that again and again, you are going to plant a seed, grow a tree, and bear forth fruit. That fruit is going to be very bitter in your life. That tree in your garden is one that satan will use again and again, not only to poison your life, but also the lives of others.

When you get this concept, generational curses begin to make so much sense.

THREE WAYS CURSES ARE ESTABLISHED

CHAPTER 03 – THREE WAYS CURSES ARE ESTABLISHED

I always wondered why generational curses are so strong. We think that it is just a curse carried on from generation to generation, but it is a lot more than that.

A generational curse is a sin that is carried on from generation to generation. I want you to use your archetype, country, nationality, and family as an example here. Follow me closely.

A child is born to a family that has a curse of poverty on it. How is that child going to grow up? He is going to grow up thinking that God is punishing him. He is going to think that if he serves the Lord, then he is going to be poor. That is certainly what I grew up thinking.

That is the doctrine, right? If you are going to serve the Lord, you are going to be poor. That is the doctrine that was passed down through my generations. Now, when you are born, you grow up under the covering of your parents.

They already have this nice, big tree, and when their child is born, they feed that child the fruit from the tree that they have. So, you are already in bondage from their curse. You are already walking in poverty.

1. GENERATIONAL CURSES

There is something about walking under a curse that begins to shape the way you think. Children that grow up in a home that is always in poverty struggle to imagine themselves being wealthy.

Sure, they may have a successful fantasy life, but in reality, they battle to think that God would possibly bless them. They battle with impossibility thinking. Why? It is because the curse that is on their parents conditions the way that they think.

However, not even then are they in bondage completely. They still have the ability to break free of that if they would just not follow in the same family sin. Yet, one day when that child is old enough to individuate and decide for themselves, they have a choice to take on that belief system from their family, or they can take on the Word of God and believe that instead.

THE DAY YOU MAKE IT YOUR OWN

Now, it is not like you sit down one day and have this whole psychological debate. It is actually a decision that happens instantly when you are faced with a specific situation. There comes a time in your life when you make that generational curse your own.

There is a time when you not only take on the sins of your father, but you make those sins your own. You continue the sin for yourself. You can see this in many families.

You see it in families where there is sexual impurity, and you see it move from father to son. You see it in children who were beaten when they were brought up, and then they grow up and beat up their own children. They continue the sin.

There needs to come a time when somebody along that line does not just break free, but stops sinning. They must make themselves accountable and say, "Today, this sin stops here."

That is what Daniel was doing as he fasted and prayed. What was he doing? He was crying out on behalf of the sins of his people. He was saying, "Today Lord, that sin stops here. It stops with me. I will bow down to no other God but you. Today, the sin stops with me."

When you do that as a believer, you take away the license that satan has used from generation to generation to destroy you and steal your blessing. You do not have to continue the curses of your forefathers.

I have begun to understand more why re-parenting is becoming so powerful in the Church right now. It is because our minds need to be reconditioned. We have been conditioned to sin and to expect the curse, the poverty, and the suffering.

YOUR SPIRITUAL DNA

We have spiritual DNA that is contaminated with the bitter fruit of our parents that needs to be torn out. We not only need to deal with the sin, but we need to change the way that we think.

We need to get rid of the thinking that houses the sin, the thinking that makes that sin so much easier to keep doing. That is why generational curses are one of the most difficult to deal with.

We minister to a lot of people, and I would daresay that dealing with generational curses is one of the strongest curses to deal with because it is not just about the sin of their parents. It is also not just about the fact that they continued on in that sin themselves either.

It is about the point that their entire mind is conditioned toward that sin. Their upbringing, their experiences, and the doctrine that they were taught from home again and again have geared them to continue in that sin.

No wonder the Word says that we should be transformed by the renewing of our minds (Romans 12:2). However, in all of this, there is still no excuse for sin. Even though the Father does not punish or judge you for your sin, do you really think that the devil is going to be so kind and turn a blind eye to it when he can have you right where he wants you?

You think, "It was just a little sin. I do not know why God is giving me such a hard time." It is not God that is giving you a hard time. The devil is using every ace card he can to steal, kill, and destroy and to take away every blessing from you that is your inheritance as a blood-bought child of God.

I will speak about how to deal with these generational curses, but for now, I want you to identify them.

IDENTIFY YOUR GENERATIONAL CURSES

Which ones of those curses that I listed earlier are going on in your family? What curses continue? What lack or suffering is there? It is very easy to identify this. Just think of the things that are not a blessing of God — that is the curse.

I am not talking about a once-off thing. I am talking about something that is repeated in your life again and again. You can see it in your mother, your grandmother, and your great-grandmother.

You can even see some of these things in your aunts, uncles, brothers and sisters, and also in your own life. You see this so much in racial and generational curses where that sin is repeated, especially in countries that worship idols.

The generations keep repeating the sin, and the curse remains on the land. It takes time to break free. It takes a conviction to make yourself accountable and not just say, "This is the sin of my mother or father, and that is why I am suffering."

No. There came a time when you made that sin your own, and that is why you are bound. Do not ever blame the curses in your life on someone else. You are always responsible to take that sin and put it under the blood. You do not have to be a victim.

2. THE LEAVEN — CURSES THROUGH ASSOCIATION

The second way a curse can be manifest in your life is through the leaven of others.

1 Timothy 5:22 says,

> *Do not lay hands on anyone hastily, nor share in other people's sins; keep yourself pure.*

I also love what it says in 1 Corinthians 5:5 where Paul was talking to the fornicator. Paul said,

> *Deliver such a one to Satan for the destruction of the flesh, that his spirit may be saved in the day of the Lord Jesus.*

This is interesting. He did not say that he was going to hand him over to the Lord to judge or punish him. He did not say that the Father was going to smite him.

He said that he was handing this person over to satan. In other words, in his sin, he already condemned and punished himself because satan is going to take him -

all Paul was doing was removing his covering from him and saying, "If you want the devil and want to play in the devil's playground, then you go ahead and have yourself a good time. I am getting out of here."

That is why Paul said, "Do not even associate with such a person." Back off. Do not partake of their sin. If they want to sin and think that satan will give them the reward that they want, then let them have it.

Then Paul goes on to say, in 1 Corinthians 5:6-7,

> *6 Your glorying is not good. Do you not know that a little leaven leavens the whole lump?*
> *7 Therefore purge out the old leaven, that you may be a new lump, since you truly are unleavened. For indeed Christ, our Passover, was sacrificed for us.*

He was saying, "If you keep allowing this kind of sin in your midst, if you have compassion for it and understand this sin and become a partaker of it - that leaven, that sin in their life, will start manifesting in your life too."

You are going to start sinning with the same sin, and when you do that, you are going to come under the same curse. So yes, there are curses by association. However, they just do not come upon you in any old way.

When someone is walking in a curse, and you open your heart to excuse that sin, be a party to that sin, or in any way identify with that sin by saying, "Shame

shame, you poor thing. You are sinning and you cannot help it", then you just got a little bit of leaven in your dough. It does not take a lot of yeast to begin making that dough rise.

If you just put a little yeast in when you are baking bread, it spreads through the dough like crazy.

Let's say you have a mentor, friend, brother or sister, and they are going through a hard time and are really battling with anger. They share with you about how this person makes them angry and all the terrible things that were done to them that brought on the anger. Before you know it, you are taking on some of their leaven.

You are fellowshipping with them and opening your heart, and since you so need them to understand you, that leaven starts to work your lump. Next thing you know, you are walking along, and you are getting really irritated with people. You feel yourself getting angry and frustrated.

Guess what just happened? You just picked up a contamination, and you made their sin your own. That sin became an influence in your life. So, now do you go and smack that person around?

No. You need to deal with the beam in your own eye first before you go and take the splinter out of your brother's eye. Understand that what was just a little leaven has now become a beam that you need to deal with first.

DEAL WITH YOUR CONTAMINATION

You need to deal with that contamination and the fact that you succumbed to that temptation yourself and ended up walking in the same sin that they walked in. Deal with that first, and then you can go to your brother and snatch them out of the fire, hating the stain of sin.

That is why Paul was so strong when he said, "Do not even fellowship with such a person." I always thought he was being mean, but actually, he was trying to protect the church.

He was concerned, because if that person was allowed to continue that way and their actions were accepted, other people would also think that this was acceptable. Then, before you know it, everyone would be taking on the system of the world, thinking that it is ok.

I am sure that you have been in a church like that where one person does something that makes you feel uncomfortable. You think, "Hmm... that does not line up with the Word. That sounds wrong. It seems like the spirit of the world."

However, everyone accepts it, and that leaven starts to run its way among the congregation. Before you know it, everyone is doing it, and it has become perfectly all right. When that happens, it is not only the sin that is the problem, but also the consequences of the sin that are the problem.

It is the curse, the fruit that follows afterwards. You start seeing things go wrong afterwards, and the curse that was on that person ends up on you.

CONTAMINATION AFFECTS MANY

It was much like Gehazi who decided to take hold of the cursed objects and ended up getting leprosy as a result. You go there thinking that you will just do this one little sin and open up one little door, but you end up doing the same thing that they did.

So yes, when you open the door through sharing the sin of someone else, not only do you take on their sin, but you take on the curse that they are under as well. You take on the spirit of theft, strife and vain glory, loss, and sickness.

Have you ever wondered how some ministers end up getting sick just like the people that they prayed for? It is because they did not deal with the person's sin. Sometimes Jesus did not deal with their sin, but many times, He did.

That is why the Word says that He gave Himself to no man. They minister to all these people, and they never deal with the sin. They say, "Shame, you poor thing. You cannot help it that you sinned."

That leaven starts to work its way into their lives, and before you know it, they have the same disease as the people they minister to, because they did not see that the open door all along was sin.

That is why people can get prayed for again and again, get healed, and then get sick again. Why? It is because of the curse. It is because they did not close the door to the curse.

Faith can move mountains, and with faith you will surely get healed. However, you can get healed twenty times a day and then get sick again twenty times a day, until you patch up that hole that satan is getting through.

He has license in your life through sin and curses, generational curses that you have made your own, and curses by association that you have made your own.

3. THE STAIN OF SIN

Then, most importantly, the third way a curse will manifest is from your own stain of sin. Romans 6:16 says,

> *Do you not know that to whom you present yourselves slaves to obey, you are that one's slaves whom you obey, whether of sin leading to death, or of obedience leading to righteousness?*

Throughout our lives, we face rejection, hard times, poverty, lack, sickness, and people being mean to us. What decision did you make when you had that hard time? When you were rejected, abused, or hurt, and the emotions were high, and it was the first time that you had ever experienced that thing, how did you respond in that moment?

A CLOSER LOOK AT YOUR DECISIONS

What decision did you make in your heart? Whatever decision you make in your heart, you form a template. Every time that circumstance comes upon you thereafter, do you know what you are going to do? You are going to respond with that same sin.

So, you are at school, right? You are a cute little five or six-year-old, and mommy says that you are the best girl in the world, so you think that everyone else thinks so too. Then, you go to school and discover that what the rest of the world thinks and what mommy thinks is not always the same.

You go to the playground to play with the kids, and instead of them being nice to you, they tease you because of your freckles, glasses, or braces. They start pulling on your pigtails, kicking your shins, or beating you up after school - it hurts, and it's horrible.

It is a devastating experience, and in that moment, you are going to make a decision without even thinking. "Am I going to turn the other cheek, or am I going to respond with bitterness?"

It really depends on the person. It does not matter what happens to you in life - it matters how you deal with it. I have seen people that have been abused in ways that I cannot begin to imagine, yet they have the most positive outlook on life.

Why? It is because when those things happened to them, they chose not to sin and chose to walk in righteousness. As a result, those things did not remain a bondage in their lives.

Then, I have seen others who barely had someone say a bad word to them, and they got so bitter and angry that they became a very nasty person to be around. Whatever decision you make in that moment lays a foundation for your life, especially in the early, formative years.

THE ROOT QUICKLY FORMS A TREE

When you commit that sin for the first time, in that experience, every time you face a similar experience, you are going to respond with the same sin. Suddenly, your mind starts to go back to the fight with your wife that you had the other week.

What do you know? You are sinning in the same way that you did when you were five years old. Then, you wonder why you have poverty in your life. You wonder why there is adultery and why your relationships are being torn apart.

It is because you have a curse. You opened a door to the enemy through your sin, a sin that you have repeated again and again.

Everyone actually likes generational curses because then they have someone to blame. "Well, my mom was a bad mom. She passed on some bad things to me, so it is all her fault."

What about the sin that you nurtured since you were a child? The sad part is that you end up sowing the seed, nurturing the tree, and producing the fruit, and then your children will eat that fruit too.

One day, you will give birth to those gorgeous little ones. They will grow up, and you will see manifesting in them the very thing that you never wanted to see in anyone ever again.

You see character traits - bad ones, sinful ones in them. You see curses. You think, "He is accident prone, just like me. He has cancer, just like me." They are eating your fruit, and now they are paying the price for your sin.

That is another reason why you should deal with the curses in your life. You have a whole lot of leaven in your lump, and you contaminate others with your leaven.

Everyone that agrees with your sin, opens their heart to you, loves you, and receives from you - gets contaminated by your sin. It manifests a curse in their lives. So, the stain of sin spreads.

However, there is a solution for sin. You do not have to stay bound. You do not have to stay stuck in it. How long does it take to say, "Father, forgive me. I wash this sin with the blood of Christ."?

INNER HEALING — UNCOVERING THOSE ROOTS

That is why when you do inner healing, you will deal a lot with personal sin, demonic bondages, and the curses in people's lives. Usually, it is in those difficult times that we make wrong choices.

Who is going to get bitter when someone gives them one hundred dollars? You are not going to get bitter about that unless you have more problems than the ones I am talking about in this book.

If you are a prophet, you are going to be dealing with this a lot. You are going to see curses manifesting in people's lives. Then, when you pray, the Lord will show them to you when they were at the age of five.

You will think, "Lord, I was praying about why they are crashing their car, and then you show me them at the age of five. Why did You do that?" It is because that is when the sin started.

In that experience, at that age in their life, they made a wrong decision, a sinful decision that they have continued since then. It has been an open door in their life. They need to put that sin under the blood and get forgiveness for it. Then they need to tell the devil to get lost because he is using that as an access point to destroy them.

CHAPTER **04**

The Difference Between Curses and Spiritual Warfare

CHAPTER 04 – THE DIFFERENCE BETWEEN CURSES AND SPIRITUAL WARFARE

I am going to look very quickly at the difference between curses and spiritual warfare. I put this in because it is valid for those that are saying, "If everything is a curse, then when does spiritual warfare come in?"

THE ARROWS – A PICTURE OF SPIRITUAL WARFARE

This also confused me. Now, remember when I shared with you the picture of the city and the walls? I told you that the hole in the wall is a symbol of the curse. Well, arrows are a symbol of spiritual warfare.

Spiritual warfare is the external attack of the enemy. That is when people pray against you, speak against you, and the enemy decides to wear you down and accuse you in order to make that wall crumble and crack.

What the enemy is really trying to do is to get you to sin. Spiritual warfare has one intention. It is to get you to allow a hole in your wall. However, the Scripture says that we need to stand with a shield of faith.

When those attacks come against you, the enemy comes with his lies and accusations, and all the hordes of hell are loosed against you, you do not have to be afraid.

You just stand with the shield of faith and say, "No. I am not succumbing to fear, bitterness, or any of this. I stand in the name of Jesus, and I send back those arrows. They are not coming anywhere near my wall."

> **Proverbs 25:28** *Whoever has no rule over his own spirit is like a city broken down, without walls.*

THE CRACK IN THE WALL - YOUR PERSONAL SIN

Yet, what if someone is speaking against you, and you get bitter at them? You just dug yourself a hole in your wall, did you not? All those words and those curses that they are speaking over you are going to have an effect.

> **Proverbs 26:2** *Like a flitting sparrow, like a flying swallow, so a curse without cause shall not alight.*

When you "give that curse a cause", it will strike you. Those arrows are going to get through your wall if you allow yourself to fall into sin or get bitter, angry, or frustrated. Spiritual warfare is all about satan trying to trip you up. You do not need to partake of the curses of others – just do not give that curse any cause. Spiritual warfare tries to trick you into giving that curse a cause (through sin)!

Is that not what he did in the Garden of Eden to trick Eve? He threw those arrows at her, but it was only when she ate the fruit that she sinned. That is what spiritual warfare is. It is warfare coming against you to get you to fail. That is why the Scripture says to bless and not curse.

It says in Romans 12:14,

> *Bless those who persecute you; bless and do not curse.*

So, how do you overcome spiritual warfare? You bless! You send those arrows back in the name of Jesus. You speak forth the blessing of God and make sure that there are no little holes, ditches, or cracks in that wall for those arrows to get through.

You say, "In the name of Jesus, I stand against those words, and I speak faith, hope, and love. I will not be moved. This heart will not be affected by those words. This soul will not be discouraged because of what they said."

The minute it does, you allow those arrows to get in. When you allow those arrows into your life, that is when they will destroy you. However, you do not have to experience this. That is the biggest difference between spiritual warfare and curses.

Spiritual warfare is the attack that comes from without - it is the arrow sent by the enemy through his agents that are only too willing to speak those words. In other words, if someone is praying against you, their prayers have no power, unless you allow them to.

You allow that power by getting bitter and frustrated at them. All you need to do is stand behind that shield of faith and remain in the spirit and in His blood, and those arrows will not touch you.

The scripture above in Proverbs 26 says that the curse will not alight. It will not have any power over you. He has delivered you from every curse, the curse of the people, and the curse of their words. They cannot touch you... if you remain in Christ.

NO NEED TO FEAR

Does that not set you free? We have it backwards. I have people always travailing about, "This person is speaking a curse on me, putting voodoo and witchcraft on me, and another person is praying against me."

Who cares? They cannot touch me. I am a blood-bought child of God. Check it out. The blood of Christ is all over me. You can't touch this! Christ did not die in vain. Yet, we sure act like it sometimes.

"I am so afraid that someone is going to put a curse on me..."

Give me your best shot. Check out what happens when you try to curse me. I do not need to deal with you because God has it under control.

> *Genesis 12:3 I will bless those who bless you, and I will curse him who curses you; and in you all the families of the earth shall be blessed.*

He said that He would bless those that bless me and curse those that curse me. You are not just coming against me. So, if you want to curse me, bring it on. That curse will bounce right back at you because God Himself will take that arrow and pierce it into your own heart.

So please, knock yourself out. I am not going to sit and travail over every single person that prays against this ministry because I do not need to. By cursing me, they sin, and in their sin, they undo themselves.

Why do I need to fret about it? What I do need to fret about is my own heart. I need to make sure that I do not get all stressed and bitter. "I am such a nice person. How could they say that?"

You just let that arrow through. You succumbed to the temptation, and now you will experience that warfare at a whole new level. I hope that set you free because satan has been getting in, but not in the places that you think.

The place that you left unattended is where he is actually sneaking through. I have two simple definitions that I want to share with you here:

Curses – the fruit of un-repented, repetitive sin

Spiritual Warfare – an onslaught of the enemy designed to discourage you and make you sin

We have an answer for both of those, and they both begin and end with the blood of Christ.

STEP-BY-STEP SOLUTIONS

CHAPTER 05 – STEP-BY-STEP SOLUTIONS

So, how do you break through to victory? How do you deal with generational curses? A good place to start would be to identify them in the first place. Trust me, when you ask the Lord to show you, He will show you.

For many people, they see the curses. In fact, even the world sees it. They just call it hereditary sickness and disease. We know what that is. It is a curse that has been passed down from generation to generation.

DEALING WITH GENERATIONAL CURSES

STEP 1: TAKE OWNERSHIP

What habits are you doing that were the same as your forefathers? Ladies and gentlemen, if you see a generational curse in your life, it is time to take ownership of it. There is something very powerful about that, and I am speaking from my own experience.

When I said, "This is my father's curse, my grandfather's curse, or my father's sin," I always felt so powerless to do something about it. I felt like the boxer in 1 Corinthians 9 hitting the air.

I never felt like I was connecting with satan's jaw. I was just punching around trying to do warfare against everything in order to get a victory. Then, one day the

Lord said, "You take ownership and responsibility for this sin."

Remember that old song, "It's not my mother or my sister, but it's me, oh Lord, standing in the need of prayer"? The Lord brought me to my knees and said, "You take ownership. This is not their curse or any of your ancestors' curse. It is your curse."

I permitted this in my life. All I needed to do was apply James 4:7 to my life. *"Therefore submit to God. Resist the devil and he will flee from you."* Once you have taken ownership, you are holding that sin in your hand, and guess what?

You can put it under the blood and wash it away. While it is your dad's sin, your mom's sin, or your grandfather's sin, you cannot do anything with it. I cannot wash away their sin. That is for Christ to do, not me.

However, I can bring my sin to Christ. I can put my responsibility under the blood and be redeemed. I can ask for forgiveness, and I can submit to the Lord. So, that is what you need to do.

STEP 2: APPLY THE BLOOD

You say, "Father, forgive me for I have sinned. Yes, we may have a curse of poverty in my family, but Lord, there was a time when I blamed you for that poverty. That was sin.

There was a time when you told me to walk in faith, but I did not. I walked in fear, and that which is not of faith is sin. Father, forgive me for not walking in faith. Forgive me for doubting you. Forgive me for blaming you and getting bitter towards you.

By getting bitter and angry, I made that sin my own, and I brought that curse upon myself. I repent Father. Satan, I close that door, and I chop down this tree. You will get out of my life right now.

I remove the spirit of poverty, and I tell it to be gone in Jesus' name. I am not accepting it anymore."

STEP 3: RENEW YOUR MIND

When people are dealing with generational sins and curses, I tell them that, for the first while, they will probably have to pray about it daily. Why? It is because that curse shaped the way you think.

It is not good enough even after praying and repenting. You have to stop thinking that way. You have to stop giving that soil fertilizer for the seed to keep growing. The way that you think and act keep leading you down this sinful road.

You have to be transformed by the renewing of your mind. If you want to break free of generational curses, be transformed by the renewing of your mind. Think a different way, and you will not keep falling into the same sin again and again.

Sure, you could just stand against that sin in your willpower. You can do it, but it is going to be hard. It is easier to say, "Lord, change me. Let me be clay on the potter's wheel. Change the way I think, so that I do not think this way anymore.

Give me a new way. Replace my doubt with faith, and my fear with love. Replace this thinking that says that it is you doing these bad things to me. Replace these things with the truth so that I can be set free Lord."

When you do that, not only will you break free of the generational sin, but you will also not pass it onto the generations after you. You will become a different person. For those of you in apostolic training - a lot of this should be making sense.

Suddenly, you understand why the Lord said that He wants you to let go of family and let go of your country. Why does the Lord do that to apostles? It is because you need to break free of those generational sins.

You cannot keep passing them onto your children, spiritual or natural. You have to break free, which means that you have to become a different person so that you do not fall into the same trap again and again.

So, put your sin under the blood, and tell the enemy to flee. Then, let the work begin, and start changing your habits so that you do not keep doing the same thing that you have been doing.

CHANGE - THE KEY TO VICTORY

What has been happening up until now? You sin, and then you repent and tell the devil to go. Then you sin again. If you keep going on like that, you will get victory, but that is like running a race with your feet tied together.

You are going to exhaust yourself. Why don't you just change? Then, you will not sin in the same way anymore, and you will not have this curse anymore. It is easy. Just stop doing that thing you keep doing that keeps opening the door to the enemy.

Every time you do that thing, you give flight to the curse. You think, "Perhaps, no one saw me sin?" Well, someone did see it. The devil is only too glad when you fall into your usual sin trap. So, stop it, and change who you are.

If you keep falling into the same sin again and again in a certain environment, get into another environment. Have a mentor get on you to change and put pressure on you. Get a spiritual parent that can give you another way to think and act, so that you can deal with the sin in you and deal with those sinful mindsets.

That is how you deal with generational curses.

DEALING WITH LEAVEN

STEP 1: BREAK SPIRITUAL LINKS

Now, when it comes to dealing with leaven, you have to disassociate yourself spiritually from your brother that is not walking in the light. That does not mean that you need to reject him.

It means that you love him, but you are not going to take his nonsense. It is like Jude 1:22-23 says,

> *22 And on some have compassion, making a distinction;*
> *23 but others save with fear, pulling them out of the fire, hating even the garment defiled by the flesh.*

Love them, but hate the stain of sin because the stain of sin is like a contaminate or mold. It is leaven that spreads and destroys. It brings all twenty of those curses that I spoke about.

SIN MUSTN'T BE "LOVED"

People have this strange idea in both the world and in the church. "If you really love me, you would understand. You would just accept that this is the way that I am."

The truth is - I love you. I hate the stain of sin.

The Bible does not say that I have to love your sin. I am sorry, but the Bible says that I have to love you, and I do. I love this little quirkiness about you. I love your heart for the Lord. I love how you always make me laugh and that you are always there for me.

I love you, but I hate your rebellion, your jealousy, your fornication, and your adultery. I do not have to love your sin. The Bible does not tell me to love your sin.

The minute you accept and receive someone's sin, you receive the curse along with it. That is why it is so important when you have received a contamination from someone to search your own heart. Why are you so quick to agree with their sin and be a partaker of it?

Is there something that you need? Are you looking to them to meet a need in your heart that only the Lord can meet? Are you looking to this person to accept you in only a way that the Lord can accept you?

STEP 2: IDENTIFY YOUR NEED

Do you have a take/take relationship with this person? If so, that is your open door right there. No one should be meeting that need except the Lord. This is probably one of the biggest ways to pick up a curse from someone else. It is by needing them for something only the Lord can give you.

As believers, we should always be pouring and giving out. This is actually one of the easiest curses to deal with. Do you know what usually happens? You meet an old friend, and you chat and share. The time was so good, but then on your way home, your car breaks down.

Once you get home, your stove blows up, and then your child calls you. They are sick at school. You think, "What just happened? Out of the blue, so many things just started going wrong."

You just took on a bit of leaven. That is what happened. It is very easy to deal with this. You just need to break links. "Father, I disassociate myself with that sin. In Jesus' name, I speak blessing on that person, but I do not accept that sin.

I pray, Holy Spirit, that you take them where they need to go and that you deal with them accordingly so that they can come in line, but I am not partaking and fellowshipping with that sin. I am not bringing it into my home and making it a part of my life."

It does not mean that you reject them, but you certainly do not accept or feel sorry for their actions, because every one of us in this world has the freedom to choose. They can choose to sin or not to sin.

Each of us walks out our own walk before God in fear and trembling. It is not for you to walk their road. It is for them to walk their road. Leave them to walk it, and you walk yours.

DEALING WITH PERSONAL SIN

Then, there is dealing with personal sin. Again, this one is very easy. You see your sin, and you see the pattern through your life. You always responded to the same thing in the same way.

STEP 1: GO BACK TO THE BEGINNING AND REPENT

Go back to the very first thing that happened and repent. "Lord, when those kids were bullying me, I know that I made a judgment in my heart. I know that I wanted to turn around and punch them in the nose.

I was so angry, so violently angry. Forgive me Lord, because every time I am under pressure, I respond the same way. I always respond in bitterness. Forgive me Lord."

If there is someone that you can pray with, have them go into those memories with you, and speak the healing as well. Say, "Satan, that door that I gave you access through, I close it. You loose your hold, and get out of here."

STEP 2: CHANGE YOUR HABITS

Then, change your habits. When you find yourself in that same situation and feel that temptation to respond in the same way, do not do it. If you really want to break free, in the heat of the moment, make a new decision. Create a new righteous template, instead of a sinful one, and you will break free.

The great thing is that the blessing of the Lord is like a river in flood, and the curses that the enemy uses are like a beaver dam that blocks up that blessing. If you just take down the dam, that river will flow.

Here you are, thinking that you have to travail and beg God for His blessing, but He is telling you to simply stand under the waterfall. His blessing is there. You have access to His storehouse.

Deal with the curses, and the blessing will come naturally. You do not have to keep begging God to bless you. He has blessed you with every blessing. When Jesus went to the cross, He gave you everything that the Father has.

You do not have to keep asking God for blessing. You have to figure out what is stopping that blessing. You have to put it under His blood, and then the blessing will flow again. If you are experiencing curses in your life, then deal with them, and walk in blessing.

PRACTICAL PROJECT

1. Make a list of the curses in your life from the twenty that I named in Chapter 2. Which category do they fall into?

    a. Personal Sin

       i.   You are the only one in your family who has it

      ii.   You are the only one out of everyone you know who has it

    iii.   The only other people you see it in are your children

   b. Generational Curses

       i.   Pattern in your family

      ii.   Had it before you can remember

    iii.   Was always with you

    iv.   Grew into it

   c. Leaven of Others

       i.   Curse manifested after being with someone

      ii.   Old friends, ministers, mentors... someone you submitted to

2. Identify when each one of these curses began.

3. Repentance

I do not know about you, but there is nothing like a good conviction. It helps you to break free and let go of those loads. There is no greater feeling than to be able to come to the cross and lay those loads down, especially when the enemy has been accusing you, you have been having doubts, and people have been speaking against you. You just feel so loaded down.

When that happens, there is a temptation to try and justify yourself. You should rather run to the cross and repent. It only takes five minutes. His blood is always there, and it is always available to you.

If it is a personal sin, ask the Lord to forgive you. Go back to where you first started this pattern in your life, where you repeated the same sin, and ask Him for forgiveness.

Identify that open door, and actually, you should take time daily to repent. Matthew 6:9-13 says,

> *9 In this manner, therefore, pray: Our Father in heaven, hallowed be Your name.*
> *10 Your kingdom come. Your will be done on earth as it is in heaven.*
> *11 Give us this day our daily bread.*
> *12 And forgive us our debts, as we forgive our debtors.*
> *13 And do not lead us into temptation, but deliver us from the evil one. For Yours is the kingdom and the power and the glory forever. Amen.*

It goes on to say that if you do not forgive your brother, God will not forgive you. In other words, ask for forgiveness for your sins, and forgive others as well. This is a daily prayer.

Seeking the Lord for His blessing every day is so simple. Lay those sins down. It does not have to be a whole big travail. Just put them under the blood. Don't do it because God needs you to. He got the memo two thousand years ago.

It's you who needs to put those sins under the blood, so that your heart is no longer condemned, and you can go to the Throne with boldness.

Also, you need to do it so that satan does not have a foothold in your life. Is that not worth it? Then, when you are repenting of generational sins, take ownership of them, identify when you made the curse your own, and repent.

The same goes for the leaven of others. Find out where you opened the door, where you allowed that sin into your life, and get yourself a new lump. Ask the Lord to purge you, to help you to let go and see through His eyes, and to minister and bless His people effectively.

Quick Note on Doctrine

I also want to mention that the leaven of others also includes teachings that you receive in your spirit from people that were not exactly in right standing with God. This comes from doctrines that were heretical or teachings from someone who has a contamination in their spirit.

When you receive those things in your life, you walk in the curse as well. You can simply say, "Lord, forgive me for getting into that teaching. I should not have done that. I knew better than to watch that movie or to receive that thing into my heart."

It does not have to be a drama. This is a daily, simple thing. That is the balance that I hope to bring about curses. I know that this is very intense and can be broken down in so many different parts, but more than anything, I want to leave you with hope.

You do not have to suffer anymore. You do not have to be poor anymore. You do not have to be sick anymore, and you do not have to pass these things down to your children.

You have the power in His blood to stop it dead in its tracks. So, do that. Lay the axe to those roots. Wash out the stain of sin that is in your life, and you will walk in the abundance of blessing that God has given to you as an inheritance.

TEARING DOWN
STRONGHOLDS

CHAPTER 06 – TEARING DOWN STRONGHOLDS

After the previous chapters, I spent much time in prayer every day with my husband, Craig, and we held the ministry up to the Lord.

As we dealt with personal sin and all the principles that I shared with you, in the spirit, I saw our ministry as a city on a hill. I saw that we had patched up every last open door and every crack in our walls. The city was secure.

Then, it was as if I was standing on the city wall looking at the land surrounding us. The Lord said to me, "Colette, it is not good enough for you to just possess the city. I want you to go and take the land.

I want you to take back the land that satan has stolen from my people. I don't just want you to take back the land that I have given you, but I want you to go beyond that and take his land as well for my Kingdom, in my name."

As I continued to pray and step out onto this land, beyond the boundary of our city, our realm, and our little world, I saw in the distance these machines of war that the enemy had set up.

In the spirit, what gave me a bit of caution, was that these weapons of warfare that he had established were securely built and entrenched in the land. In fact, it looked as if they had been cemented into the land surrounding our city.

This was a place where satan continued to attack us again and again, from the same vantage point. I said, "Lord, what is this a picture of?"

He said, "This is a picture of the strongholds of the enemy. Sure, the enemy cannot steal from you if you do not let him in your walls. If you do not allow the cracks, he cannot come in.

However, there are these strongholds that the enemy has in your life where he attacks you again and again, from that same vantage point that cause you to lose your faith.

He causes you to become rattled, to sin, and let your guard down for just a moment so that he can get in."

When I got that revelation, my husband and I put our hearts and prayers towards tearing down those strongholds. We started doing spiritual warfare at a level that we never had before.

So, this chapter is borne from that because we got such a victory and breakthrough by tearing these strongholds down in our lives. I know that as you learn to tear these strongholds down in your life, you will get the victory as well.

Satan cannot attack you unless he has license. That is already something that you know. I taught you that in chapter 1. However, you need to realize that he will come at you from without, and he will use these strongholds to challenge your faith, hope, and love so that you will let him in.

This is what we are going to do. Instead of just putting up the shield and blocking those attacks again and again, we are changing tactics on the enemy and going to become offensive in our warfare.

OFFENSIVE WARFARE BEGINS HERE

We are going to march down to the middle of that field where he has set up those strongholds, and we are going to tear them down. This way, he cannot rattle us anymore and tempt us to lower our guard.

Why keep blocking when you can go straight to the source and stop the attack in the first place? How much warfare do we do that is defensive?

"Lord, please help me get better because I am already sick. Please help my finances because I am already broke."

That is defensive warfare. We have to go a step beyond this and get a hand up on the enemy. We have to stop saying, "Please, please and sorry, sorry" and go down there, tear down those strongholds, and take that land back for ourselves. Then, take it even further and take the land that he has as well.

According to the Word, that land belongs to the righteous. You and I are the righteous. That land belongs to us in the name of Jesus.

NAMING THE STRONGHOLDS

What are these strongholds? These next principles exploded in my spirit.

Ephesians 6:12, 16 says,

> *12 For we do not wrestle against flesh and blood, but against principalities, against powers, against the rulers of the darkness of this age, against spiritual hosts of wickedness in the heavenly places.*
>
> *16 above all, taking the shield of faith with which you will be able to quench all the fiery darts of the wicked one.*

It is not your pastor that you have to fight. It is not your wife, your husband, your boss, or the person that keeps talking about you behind your back. This is not where your warfare is coming from.

Your warfare is coming from these strongholds of the enemy. He is sending those fiery darts from those weapons of warfare, in that stronghold, against your city. So, let's march down and remove those strongholds.

However, before we can do that, let's have a look at what these strongholds are. I am going to deal with three main strongholds. You will find every work that the enemy does in your life hangs on these three main strongholds.

You will find that every other temptation that he brings to you to cause you to slip and fall are on these three strongholds.

These three strongholds are: fear, guilt, and bitterness.

We have dealt with our sin. We know that it is wrong to hate. We know that it is wrong to not have faith in the Lord. We know that it is wrong to take our eyes off the goal and the promise, and to put our eyes on ourselves.

We have dealt with the sin and pleaded the blood morning, noon, and night. You have obeyed God and walked in repentance, and you are saying, "Lord, there is no more death to be done in me. I have been crucified ten times over."

However, when you realize that these three strongholds are not just sin, but weapons of warfare that satan attacks you with, it changes your perspective. You start realizing that you can send back the fiery darts of the enemy.

SATAN'S COUNTERFEIT

What we have here, in these three strongholds, is the counterfeit to the power of God - namely, faith, hope, and love.

If you are familiar with our teachings, you will hear again and again that it is not about you doing everything in your strength or God doing everything in His strength. Rather, it is about God manifesting His will on this earth through the agency of man.

In other words, it is a relationship - a partnership. God works through us to get things done in this world. I think there are very few people that would disagree with that statement.

MAN'S PART TO PLAY

Did you really think that satan would just stand on the sideline and let God have all the fun? He has been imitating and trying to mock God since the beginning of time. Is it any surprise that the father of all lies would want a counterfeit of his own?

Do you know what happens when satan wants something done in this earth? He gets a man to help him out. When these strongholds are established, satan's will is carried out when satan works with man.

I wish that I could say that God is always the one working in and through me. Yes, sinless perfection is our goal and destination, but how many times have bitterness, fear, and guilt caused us to fall so that it becomes satan working with man?

Instead of working out and walking out God's plan in our lives, and in this world, we end up doing the complete opposite and fulfill the enemy's work in our lives. That is why we have to tear these strongholds down.

OPPOSING FAITH, HOPE, AND LOVE

God gave man dominion in this earth. So, whose plan are we going to fulfill? Are we going to walk in faith, hope, and love, or in fear, guilt, and bitterness?

Depending on which one you take hold of, the result will determine the level of success you walk in, and whether or not God's promises are fulfilled in your life.

Faith, hope, and love, make things happen on this earth. They take what is in the heavenly realm, and they make it manifest on the earth.

Faith moves mountains. Hope is the focus that causes you to reach your goal, and love is the key that unlocks the promises of God's Word.

Faith, hope, and love are the three "doing" words of God.

They make us do what we should be doing at the right time that we should be doing it and in the right spirit that we should be doing it in.

So, if satan can counteract each one of these, we end up retracting the power that each one of them could be manifesting in our lives. Then, instead, we walk in loss, theft, works of the flesh, and every evil thing.

I have already done some teaching on how you can build faith, hope, and love. In *Hope – The Power of Focus*, I shared how you need to have focus and how you build the three pillars of hope to head towards your goal.

HOW YOU BUILD A "STRONGHOLD" FOUNDATION

So, let's go back a bit. How do you build these stronghold foundations? How do they come about in the first place?

It starts with that little sin that I spoke about in The Stain of Sin chapter. It starts with one little bitterness, one little fear, and one little guilt where you slipped up and failed, and guess what? It forged a little foundation.

That in itself is not such a bad thing, except the minute that this happens, satan catches wind of the fact that you have a weakness for this particular circumstance.

Let's take fear as an example. You are a young child and get sick, and then you are afraid of getting sick again. If satan wants you to keep feeling fear, he just needs to hint at sickness and has you right where he wants you.

In that moment, you feel as Apostle Paul did when he cried out to the Lord saying, "Lord, I have this thorn in my flesh that satan keeps buffeting me with."

That is what happens when we sin the first time and start that first link in the chain. It forms a foundation in our lives and gives us a limp like Jacob had. It gives us a weakness, a tender spot, where satan can push again and again, just to see us jump.

Every time we jump and respond to that influence, we give satan a brick that he uses to build that stronghold. Before long, that little weakness of yours is growing, and it is a huge, big stronghold.

Now, satan just needs to give a little hint towards it, and you lose all faith, all hope, and all love.

So, let's go back to the root, and I am going to teach you to overcome each one of those strongholds individually. If you look at the warfare that you are experiencing in your life, take a good look at what you are feeling and experiencing right now. You will start realizing that it stems from one of those three things.

You either got angry and bitter at the Lord, circumstances, or people, or you feared your circumstance and what could happen. You may have felt condemned and guilty and felt like you failed the Lord, and it caused you to back off.

How Satan Builds a Stronghold — Step 1,2,3

Let's talk about the first sin that I mentioned - the one that starts the ball rolling. I want to make a quick point on how that foundation starts because it is not so obvious at first.

Let's say, for example, that you have this terrible fear of dogs. The very first time you experienced a dog attack, it gripped you with fear.

You just created a foundation there. That spirit of fear gets rooted in that foundation, and every experience that you have after that is like a brick upon a brick, building that stronghold.

Then, all satan needs to do to rattle you is throw a dog at you... and you are down. However, that is not the only way that a foundation can be built. It can also happen by taking on the sins of others.

1 Corinthians 15:33 says,

> *Do not be misled: 'Bad company corrupts good character.' (NIV)*

Proverbs 22:24-25 says,

> *24 Make no friendship with an angry man, and with a furious man do not go,*
> *25 Lest you learn his ways and set a snare for your soul.*

You can take on the strongholds of your parents because those strongholds predispose you to a weakness.

For example, if you grow up in a home where everyone is afraid of sickness, even though you try hard not to be afraid, you cannot help but be afraid because everyone else around you is afraid.

You pick up that spiritual DNA from them, and it makes you susceptible. One day, sickness comes knocking at your door, and you have a choice to make. It makes it very hard to make the right choice.

If you make the wrong choice, that foundation is created in your life. Then, satan uses that same open door to attack you, rattle you, and get you down again and again.

Perhaps, it is a doctrine that you have been taught. This can be very strongly tied with fear and condemnation. Let's say that you were taught that if you sin, you are going to hell. You heard this over and over again.

It makes you weak in this area. Then, a day comes along when you believe it for yourself, and you make that doctrine your doctrine. At that moment, you create a foundation, a thorn in the flesh that satan will use to buffet you again and again.

So, let's go back there and undo some of that.

SATAN'S BATTLEFIELD — THE MIND

2 Corinthians 10:3-5

3 For though we walk in the flesh, we do not war according to the flesh.
4 For the weapons of our warfare are not carnal but mighty in God for pulling down strongholds,
5 casting down arguments and every high thing that exalts itself against the knowledge of God, bringing every thought into captivity to the obedience of Christ

I love this scripture. Whenever satan is attacking me, and those fiery darts are coming from his machines of war, that is the scripture that I go to.

Isn't it interesting that the scripture says that the weapons of our warfare are not carnal, but mighty through God to the pulling down of "strongholds"? This is the core of this teaching.

Then, it goes on to say, "Casting down imaginations and every high thing against the glory of God." What does that have to do with strongholds?

You would think that it would be speaking about the princes of the air or princes over a country or something grand - some big "hot shot" demon that we have to go and attack. However, it talks about casting down imaginations. Why?

Listen to this very carefully. The mind is satan's battlefield. This is where he builds the strongholds. The stronghold is built in your mind - your soul. That is why the passage goes in to talking about casting down imaginations.

First Attack: Thoughts and Images

When satan starts disarming you, he does not always come as a roaring lion. He comes with attacks of fear, guilt, and bitterness... and guess where these attacks begin? They begin in your mind, which leads to your emotions, and then affects your will so that you act out that stronghold and solidify it in your life.

The attack begins in your soul. It begins with a picture in your mind. You do not want to be afraid, but you suddenly see that picture of your grandmother dying. You do not want to feel guilty, but suddenly, the pictures come back of the sin that you committed and the event that took place.

You do not want to be bitter, but suddenly, you remember what that person did to you. It is as if you are right there. Those pictures start running in your mind, and you try to push those pictures down and those thoughts away.

You try to push away that voice in your head that keeps condemning you or saying, "You do not have to take that. You should respond to them. You should get angry." You know that you should not be thinking these thoughts, but the pictures are so clear.

Second Attack: Your Emotions

Before you know it, those pictures that have been painted start bringing forth an emotion. You are trying so hard not to feel fear, but that picture is so real. That fear starts to bubble up from deep inside of you.

Then, the picture comes again, and the fear gets stronger. The end of the month comes, and the money is not there for the bills. Your mind goes back to times when there was lack.

You have pictures in your mind. You see yourself out on the street, and you see the kids with no food or clothes. You see all these pictures that satan has put in your mind, and fear starts rising up.

Then you say, "Lord, I know that you said that you would provide. I know that you said that you would heal. I know that you said that you would set me free." However, you are dwelling so much on those negative pictures that they are all you see and feel.

THIRD ATTACK: YOUR WILL DECIDES

The next thing you know, you are acting out of fear. You say, "I need to do something right now so that we can make money. I need to do something right now to make sure that my child does not get sick. I need to do something right now to cover my guilt.

I must do something right now to make sure that the person who hurt me doesn't hurt me again."

Guess what you just did? You just took your eyes off your focus. You just lost all your hope. You lost all your faith in the Lord to win the battle for you, and you certainly lost all of your love, which gives you the greatest power of all.

You find yourself running in circles and reacting. You respond with anger, and it gives you a force because you are so angry. You step out and say, "I will show them."

At that moment, that fiery dart of the enemy just caused a huge crack in your wall. You let him in to wreak havoc in your life. You run out and do something spontaneous out of fear to try and make things better.

In the end, you make things worse, because in the moment that you act on fear, you make a big crack in your wall that allows the enemy in.

You may also respond in guilt or condemnation and end up in a cycle of self-pity. Then, instead of setting your eyes on the goal, you are so busy feeling sorry for yourself and being down and discouraged, listening to the voice of the enemy, that you open up a big crack in your wall.

So, why don't we go and take down those strongholds? I have given you the mechanics of how the enemy builds those strongholds, and how they work, but let's now look at the mechanics of how to tear them down.

REMOVING SATAN'S POWER

CHAPTER 07 — REMOVING SATAN'S POWER

Repentance is a good start, but we have already dealt with that. I want to focus more on tearing down what the enemy is doing, so that he does not keep tempting you with these same sins.

FEAR — COUNTERFEIT TO FAITH

Fear is the counterfeit to faith. Try having fear and faith at the same time. I always thought that doubt was the counterfeit to faith, but actually, I can have faith and doubt at the same time.

I know that sounds crazy, but do you remember the parable in Mark 9 where a father brought his demon possessed son to Jesus and said, "Lord, give me more faith and help my unbelief"?

It is actually possible to have faith and doubt at the same time. The nagging thoughts in the back of your mind cause you to doubt your faith. However, faith still stands strong through doubt. If you push through, you can still have faith.

Yet, try to have faith and fear together. If you are lying in bed sick, panicking that you have a disease or incurable condition, you may try so hard to have faith. But when you close your eyes, you are just gripped with fear.

You know that you should have faith, and you confess that you have faith, but let's just be straight with each other. You are loaded with fear.

Fear runs rampant in your finances, future, relationships, marriage, in the world, in the church, and in your ministry. You walk in so many different fears.

The minute you do this, fear steals your faith. Do you want to know the coolest solution to dealing with fear?

James 5:16 says,

> *Confess your trespasses to one another, and pray for one another, that you may be healed. The effective, fervent prayer of a righteous man avails much.*

This is the solution to fear. Confessing your faults to each other? Yes, because the mind is the battlefield of the enemy. If you want to really deal with your fear, you need to get it out of your mind, put it into your hand, and then nail it to the cross.

NAME YOUR FEARS — SUBMIT

There is only one way to do that, and that is to confess it. People are so afraid that the things they fear will come upon them. Guess what?

When you confess your faults, your fears, and your sin to one another, you can say, "I am sinning with my fear because that which is not of faith is sin. I should have faith in the Lord, but, to be honest, I trust fear more right now. I fear more than I have faith.

"I have more faith in the devil than in the Lord. I have more faith that the enemy can destroy me than I have that God can heal me. I have more faith that satan can steal my finances than I do that God can give me some. I have more faith that satan can destroy my ministry than I do that God can raise it up."

That is sin because you are working with satan to accomplish his plan in this earth instead of with God to accomplish His plan. Perhaps you never thought of fear as sin, but it is sin. So, get it out.

Stop fighting this battle in your mind, because satan is the master in that place. He has been doing this for many years, and you are not going to break free in your mind. Confess your faults. Have a confession session, and get the battle out of your mind.

As you are confessing your fear and sitting down with another believer, you can say, "I know this fear sounds stupid, but this grips me so much that I can hardly breathe."

Just by confessing it and holding it in your hand, it takes away the fiery dart of the enemy because you get to see it for what it really is. It is so much bigger in your mind because of the pictures and the emotions, remember?

Since the enemy attacks you with pictures and emotions, he blows it out of proportion. When you actually express those pictures, you hear yourself expressing them and think, "That does not line up with the Word of God."

You knew that before, but saying it out loud releases a power - a force. This will set you free. Confession by itself is sometimes all that you need to be free.

Work Through Your Templates

However, there are also those fears that are grounded in experience. These are fears that have been established in your life through templates of the past, spiritual DNA, or fears that your parents have.

I have done a whole teaching on fear, so I am not going to labor the point here. However, go back to the first time that you experienced that fear and say, "Lord, forgive me for not trusting you in that time. Forgive me for not walking in faith."

It takes two minutes to put any of your failures under the blood, and then that is when the enemy will get running because in that stronghold, he had been using a spirit of fear to cloud your sound mind.

That is why confession is one of the greatest breakthroughs for fear. It brings the soundness of your mind back again. When you talk with other believers, in the mouths of two or three, everything can be established.

Their fervent prayer can avail much to help you break free. However, you usually stop right after that.

You need to go back to the template of the past, give it to the Lord, and see Jesus walking through the memory with you. Then, you will get healing from the negative experience, but you forget that satan has been using it as a stronghold.

BIND THE ENEMY AND RESTORE YOUR FAITH

You need to bind the enemy. Submit yourself to God, resist the devil, and then he will flee. Rebuke it, and build yourself up in the Word. Counter it with faith. Remember that fear destroys faith.

It is hard to have faith when your mind is full of fear. So get it out of your mind. Get it out in the open. Get inner healing and whatever else you need to get, and then you rebuke that spirit of fear.

By the time you are finished rebuking that spirit of fear, the scripture that is already in you will come to life. Stand on the Word and fill your mind with pictures of the Word instead of pictures of fear.

I will give you some projects at the end of this chapter that will help focus that for you.

GUILT — COUNTERFEIT TO HOPE

Guilt is the counterfeit of hope because how can you hope to do anything in this world or take hold of any of the promises of God if you feel like you do not qualify to have them?

1 John 3:20-21 says,

> *20 For if our heart condemns us, God is greater than our heart, and knows all things.*
> *21 Beloved, if our heart does not condemn us, we have confidence toward God.*

When your heart condemns you, you lose His presence. You lose focus on the goal that He has set before you, and all you are looking at is yourself. You end up in a cycle of self-pity.

Satan is the accuser of the brethren, and he loves to use guilt and condemnation. When this guilt and condemnation is a struggle in your mind, it is so noisy.

I remember when the Lord took me through this particular stronghold in my life. Trust me when I say that I preach this from experience, because every single one of these strongholds was in my life.

Guilt was probably the strongest. I could not stand up to preach without feeling guilty that I would let God down. I could not take care of my children without feeling guilty that I was not a good enough mother.

There was nothing that I did that I did not feel like I was somehow falling short. The crazy thing is that I grew up with this guilt all the time, so I did not even know it was guilt. It was such a part of me.

I only recognized it when I went into ministry. I was trying to step out and do what God told me to do, but I stumbled because I always felt guilty. For years, I would not re-watch any of my messages or re-read any of the books that I wrote because I felt like they were not good enough.

GROUNDED IN EXPERIENCE, DOCTRINE, AND DNA

I needed to be dealt with good and solid. God did not leave me there. He never left me hanging. He started dealing with this guilt that had been entrenched into me as a very young child.

Some of it was spiritual DNA, some of it was doctrine that was taught, and a whole lot of it was from my own experiences in life where I messed up badly. However, instead of running to the Lord and putting my sin under the blood, I allowed guilt to be my covering.

I did not bring my sin to the light in those times, and I did not realize what a consequence it would have on my life. I just knew that the spirit of guilt harassed me. If only I had known back then what I know now.

Through that sin and guilt, along with the doctrine and spiritual DNA, I created a foundation. Then, every time I failed and felt guilty again, another brick was added. Soon, satan had this stronghold in my life, and I did not even recognize those fiery darts that caused me to lower my guard again and again until the Lord started pointing it out to me.

I was seeking the Lord for something, and I felt so guilty about seeking Him. I thought, "Something is not right. There is something wrong with the way that I am feeling." He started taking me back through all the events of my past.

Going back and looking at those sins, I felt myself cringe. I thought, "I really messed that up." I felt so humiliated. I felt like a fool, and I just saw that I really messed up.

Then, the Lord said, "Where did you mess up?"

In some of the circumstances in the early days, I really did mess up, and that is where I let the guilt in. However, after that, I actually did not mess up. I did what God told me to do, but yet satan still attacked me with guilt, and I felt like a failure all the time.

The Lord said, "Yes, maybe certain things were sin and guilt. However, why do you feel guilty about the things that I told you to do after that?"

That was the stronghold. Satan had his stronghold, and I knew something was very wrong one day when I stood up to preach. I could not preach because I panicked the whole time that I would mess it up.

That is when I really started getting on my face before God and saying, "I cannot do this anymore." I will never forget when He started taking me back into those memories in my past.

Some of them were true. I really had messed up, and I felt guilty and bad about them. However, with some of them, there was no reason for me to be guilty at all. I did not fail. But, I needed Him to show me that, and I needed to believe Him.

I did not just need to know it for myself, but He needed to point out the right from the wrong, the truth from the lie. He had to teach my senses to be exercised to discern the difference, just like it tells us here in Hebrews.

> **Hebrews 5:14** *But solid food belongs to those who are of full age, that is, those who by reason of use have their senses exercised to discern both good and evil.*

TRANSFORMING GUILT TO HOPE

He had to teach me to eat the strong meat, like it says in this passage, so that I could see what the truth was and what the lie was. He needed to give me that revelation, and when He did, I did not cling to my own understanding. I clung to the blood of Christ.

I covered my sin over with His blood. Then, every time satan brought those pictures back of my sin, I just saw the blood there and saw Jesus saying, "Not guilty!"

For those things where I was not guilty and where I did not fail, I saw myself as a little girl clinging to the hand of Jesus. There were some nights that I lay in bed feeling like my gut was being torn apart, but I would cling to the hand of Jesus and let that picture saturate my mind.

I would see Him pick me up on His shoulder and say, "You are not guilty. This is my plan for you. Take hold of this." Instead of seeing satan's lies, I saw the face of Jesus Christ, and in His eyes, I was set free.

In that moment, I tore down that stronghold, and I will never forget the next morning when I woke up. I said to my husband, "The noise is gone." For the first time in my life the noise was gone.

I did not realize how loud that weapon of warfare against me was. Those fiery darts, those stones that he threw at my city, rattled against those walls so loudly every moment of my life - even in my dreams.

They were such a part of me growing up that when there was silence, I experienced a peace that passed all understanding. That is why the scripture says to be anxious for nothing, but in prayer and supplication, let your request be made known to God and the peace that surpasses all understanding will guard your heart and mind.

THE GREATEST POWER OVER GUILT

I got it. However, my victory was not found in trying to overcome my guilt. My victory was found in tearing down that stronghold and in grabbing the hand of Jesus.

When you feel guilty, you try to undo your own guilt and try to make yourself "not feel guilty." You even try to forgive yourself. Good luck with that. You can reason it with your mind as much as you would like.

"It is a false guilt. It is a false guilt."

I do not care how many times you tell yourself that or how many times you try to forgive yourself. Until you cling to the hand of Jesus and see that He has paid the price for both right and wrong, you will never break free of that guilt.

It will continue to be a noise and a stronghold in your life. You need to receive the Lord's forgiveness for the sins you have committed and for the guilt that you carry for sins you have not committed. You need to see yourself in the image of Christ.

Focus on Jesus and cling to His hand. Sometimes it may feel like all you are clinging to is a little scarlet thread, but that is all you need because He is strong enough to redeem you and set you free.

So, let's take away the power of guilt. Do you feel guilty? Repent. How much effort do we put into our guilt by trying to explain what we did wrong?

BLAME SHIFTING WON'T SET YOU FREE

We have a ministry center at the moment with a couple of five-year-olds and a three-year-old running around. The little three-year-old comes in with a bruise and a bump on his head, and we know that they were out in that backyard.

We saw some sticks and stones and a building project being constructed that was not as stable as it should have been. The little guy ran in crying about how he bumped his head, and the older two said, "He went there all by himself, and he threw his head down onto the piece of wood."

You and I both know the truth. What really happened is that the two older boys built a structure that they knew was not so stable, and so they said to the little guy, "Why don't you go first? Let's see if it is secure before we walk the plank."

Of course, he is just too happy to keep the older boys happy with him and then, "BAM" ...and so the story goes.

Do you know how much time these little boys spend trying to shift the guilt and explain the guilt instead of just admitting their guilt?

Do you know how much we exhaust ourselves trying to explain the guilt, instead of saying, "I'm guilty? I feel guilty. I am the worst mother. I am the worst father. I failed. I am full of sin. I am rotten, and I stink."

It feels so good to get it out. However, if you just keep it in your mind, you keep it in the battlefield of the enemy. Then, as you try to cover your guilt, you build sin upon sin.

Go look at the works of the flesh in chapter 2 again. You will be surprised how much of the works of the flesh comes from these three strongholds of the enemy.

RUN TOWARDS YOUR GUILT

When you feel guilty and do not want to face your guilt, you will end up trying to hide it. You will go and drink to hide that guilt, or sleep around to hide that guilt. You want it to go away.

You need your body to feel good. You need to feel something other than guilt. So, you go and feast on the flesh and try to do things to make this guilt go away. However, when all is quiet and you lie in bed at night, that guilt will gnaw at you.

There is such an easy solution for this, and all it takes is five minutes, no actually five seconds… "I am guilty. Jesus, forgive me."

Admit your guilt, even if it is a false guilt. The blood is not limited. Put it all under the blood. Have a dive in the blood of Christ. Whether your guilt is true or false, it does not matter. Put it all under the blood and see what comes up.

It is there to wash you clean from head to toe. Why be picky? Why are we so busy trying to explain ourselves away and around our guilt? Only when you put everything under the blood will you see what is really right and wrong.

I really thought that all my guilt was justified. I really felt guilty. I felt so guilty that I did not even want to face my guilt. Isn't that silly? I knew that I should not feel guilty, and I knew the principles of the authority and the blood of Christ.

However, I did not know what to do with that feeling, so I ran away from it and dove into ministry and into the anointing. While the anointing was there, it was great. Yet, I still had to go home at night and face that gnawing guilt in the pit of my stomach.

So, bring it to the Lord. "Father, forgive me for not being the minister that you want me to be. Forgive me for letting you down." Even if you have not let the Lord down, get His blood over you if you feel guilty about it.

Stop running away from guilt. Run towards it, take that stronghold, and shake it until its teeth rattle. Then, put it under your feet. That is how you deal with guilt. I know that accusation of the enemy. I hear that voice of his anywhere in my vicinity, and I am coming at him with the blood. I am taking him down.

When you put that guilt under the blood, you are going to get the Lord's forgiveness. If you get His forgiveness, you are going to be able to hold His hand. Why? It is because your heart will not condemn you.

Right now you cannot go to the Throne Room because your heart is condemning you so much that it keeps you back from the power of God.

BIND THE ENEMY — PICK UP HOPE

Satan has you right where he wants you. The greatest part after you have dealt with this guilt is that it suddenly dawns on you that satan has been using this to get you down.

You will think, "That dirty dog. I cannot believe it. All these years, I have been travailing over this guilt, and now the Lord shows me that I was never guilty."

That is when you will pick up that sword and destroy the work of the enemy. You will get your eyes focused again on the work of God, and you will get your hope again.

You repent and deal with that sin, put it under the blood, do what you have to do, and then do not leave your prayer room until you pick up your sword and bind satan because the Scripture says that he is the accuser of the brethren.

Bind those words, and bind that condemnation. When this has been a stronghold in your life, it does not leave overnight. For the first day or two, I felt so free, but a little while later, satan thought that he would test me.

STAND GUARD

He thought to himself, "This is a weakness that she has always had. She has had this since she was a little baby. So, let me see if it is still there. Let me be like the Roman soldier that walked up to Jesus and put a spear in her side and see if she flinches."

Do you know what happened when the Roman soldier put the spear in Jesus' side? Blood and water flowed because He was already dead. He did not flinch. Satan just wants to find out if you are going to flinch and give him another brick to build with.

He will come and tempt you again and see if you will fall for that familiar voice, that voice of condemnation in your mind, saying, "You missed it. You should not have said that. You should not have done that."

When that thought comes, rebuke him right away. Do not let sin get a foothold. When it begins to come, and you think, "I missed th…" stop right there and say, "In the name of Jesus, satan, I bind you."

That is how it is done. The minute that thought comes to your mind, do not let it get to your emotions and then to your will. Bind it right there, and stand every hour on the hour if you have to, until you have broken free.

Then, turn your eyes back to the focus and on the promise that God has given you, and you will indeed break free.

There is not a single believer that does not battle with guilt, both false and real. Both can go under the blood. Both are attacks from the enemy, and you do not have to take it. While you take it, it steals your hope.

It takes away your focus and makes you walk in circles. It tears down the very thing that God is trying to build up in your life. Tear down that stronghold, rip up its foundation, and do not give the enemy that license ever again.

BITTERNESS — COUNTERFEIT TO LOVE

Then, you move on to the third stronghold which is bitterness. I do not think it is a far reach to see that bitterness is the counterfeit to love.

James 3:16 says,

> *For where envy and self- seeking exist,*
> *confusion and every evil thing are there.*

Ephesians 4:26-27 says,

> *26 Be angry, and do not sin": do not let the sun*
> *go down on your wrath,*
> *27 nor give place to the devil.*

There is so much in Scripture that supports this that I had to narrow it down to a few twenty scriptures or so.

Bitterness is a lot like guilt, in that we do not like to look at it because it is wrapped up in hurt and in anger. Bitterness is like a thorn in the flesh where the thorn is festering and releasing poison into your body.

I had to take my son to the dentist. He got a crack in one of his teeth. It had gotten infected and formed an abscess. We did not know it until it was too late, and he was complaining of pain.

You could not even touch the side of his mouth. He would scream hysterically because everything around it had become infected. That is what bitterness looks like.

ANGER AND HURT – THE NUCLEI OF BITTERNESS

It is not just a thorn in the flesh or a little splinter in your finger. It is a thorn that releases infection into your body and causes you to be destroyed. It starts with hurt and anger, and that is why we do not identify it.

You say to someone, "You are so bitter."

"No, I am not. That person really hurt me. I am really angry about what they did."

That is the starting point of bitterness. That is the nucleus. Hurt and anger are the nuclei of bitterness. If you allow that nucleus to come alive and split, you have yourself an atom bomb of a whole lot of ugly stuff.

What you have in the end is actually a stronghold. Yes, hurt and offense are going to come. The Word says to feel sorry for the one through whom it comes (Matthew 18:7)

Life is not fair. You are going to get hurt, and you are going to get angry. Yet, you cannot allow that hurt and anger to become bitterness. It becomes bitterness when you do not let go of the hurt and anger.

When do hurt and anger become bitterness? The Scriptures say to be in a state of anger but to not sin or let the sun set on your anger. So, anger is not sin.

Sometimes we need to get angry. I get angry at the devil all the time. I get angry when I see heresy in the Church. I am a prophet - I get angry about a whole bunch of things.

BE ANGRY, BUT DO NOT SIN

There is nothing wrong with anger, especially if it is a righteous anger. However, when does it become bitterness? It becomes bitterness when you do not deal with that anger and get healing for the hurt.

Anger becomes bitterness when you do not use it to resolve your conflict. It turns into bitterness when you fail to put that anger under the blood. Anger gives us a power to deal with the problem when it arises.

However, you do not solve the problem. You let the sun go down on your wrath. You go to sleep angry, and that little splinter or crack in your tooth starts to get infected and spreads to your nervous system.

The next thing you know, you have a stronghold in your life. Then satan touches you in that area, and you start to react. It starts with one leader being mean to you where you do not let that anger go, and you nurture the hurt.

Then, another leader does it to you, your boss does it to you, and your spouse does it to you. Before you know it, you are loaded with so much poison that all satan needs to do to take your eyes off Jesus and steal your love is to just touch on that tooth.

You will jump so high shouting, "Ouch!" Then, you will be so focused on the hurt, anger, and everything that is wrong in your life that you will take your eyes off Jesus and then... satan ends up working with man.

Satan starts working with you to accomplish his bad will in your life, instead of God working with you to accomplish His good will in your life.

INNER HEALING IS ESSENTIAL

So, are you ready to go to the dentist? It is time to stop brushing away the hurt and the anger. Let's go back to your earliest memory and work your way up from there. If you start going through a memory and feel a sting or a hurt, then you have an unresolved bitterness right there.

You have unresolved anger that has become a brick in the stronghold that satan has been using to attack you. That is why fear, guilt, and bitterness are such huge open doors to the enemy. They get us to drop our guard.

Bitterness does this because we are tenderhearted. I shared in *The Crucified Life* that our hearts are not selective. God created us to love and to feel.

When satan comes with hurt, if you do not deal with that hurt correctly and get healing for it, he is going to push on that hurt again and again. He will do it until that hurt undoes and destroys you.

What you get from there is a spirit of strife and vainglory.

> **Philippians 2:3** *[Let] nothing [be done] through strife or vainglory; but in lowliness of mind let each esteem other better than themselves. (KJV)*

Isn't that crazy? You have the accusation from the enemy, the spirit of guilt and condemnation, the spirit of fear... For this you have what Philippians calls a spirit of strife and vainglory.

STRIFE AND VAINGLORY

When that bitterness starts really manifesting in your life, you are going to fight with everyone around you. You are going to fight with your kids, spouse, boss, friends, God... and even with yourself.

Strife will follow at your heels, and people will reject you. You will always end up upsetting people, and people will always end up upsetting you. There will be no peace or love.

You will try so hard to love. But if satan wants to get you to stop loving, he just makes you angry again. The next thing you know, your love has gone out the window. You act on that anger, make mistakes, and do things that you should not do.

You grab anchors that you should not grab hold of. That bitterness will cause you to go and do things to people. It will cause you to lose love for people. You will start taking care of number one. Then, because you are so busy worrying about your hurt, pain, and anger, you steal from others, instead of giving to them.

SELF LOVE

You will care more about yourself than you do for others. You will take your eyes off Christ and your fellow believers, and you will put them on yourself. You will love yourself more than anyone else.

Do you want to know where self-love and pride come from? It comes from a stronghold of bitterness in your life because you are wrapped up in nurturing your hurt and trying to handle your anger.

It is all about you and how you feel. It's all about what people have done to you and how your life is so bad. You are going to show them.... You say, "Why can't they do for me what I need them to do for me?"

There goes your love. Then, you start blaming God and saying, "You are the one that hurt me. You are the one that stole from me."

You are trying to seek the Lord for a miracle in your life. However, every time you do this, all satan needs to do is pull the string that makes you feel all hurt and angry all over again and so... he undoes you.

So, let's face it! Look at your unresolved hurt and anger. Are there any memories that make you feel, "I do not want to think about that person or that time?" If so, you have unresolved hurt and anger that needs to be dealt with.

You need to face those memories, take Jesus into those memories, and get healing for them. Get someone to stand with you, a pastor to pray it through with you. See that person through the Lord's eyes.

Come into His presence – forgive, and be forgiven.

OVERCOMING THIS STRONGHOLD ATTACK

Do not stop there. Up until this teaching, I only saw bitterness as sin. I saw it as us allowing thoughts into our hearts that we should not allow. Yes, to some degree, that is true.

Yet, never before did I see strife and vainglory as a spiritual attack. I never saw this as an attack that satan uses against us. It is funny because I spent a large part of my life dealing with any bitterness and making sure that my heart was free of it.

BITTERNESS IS NOT JUST SIN

However, it never occurred to me that satan was attacking me with it and that it was a stronghold. When I say bitterness, you think "sin." However, it is a lot more than sin. It is a spirit of strife and vainglory.

In other words, it is not just a thought that satan attacks you with, but it is an entire stronghold that he attacks you with. You can bind that thing!

Once you know that you have put that sin under the blood, have received healing from those hurts from the past, and that infection has been cleared from your spirit, you can stand in all confidence. You can face the devil, and say, "I bind you in Jesus' name!

I bind every spirit of strife and vainglory, and I cast down every imagination and every high thing that exalts itself against the glory of God. I bring every thought into captivity."

Time to Engage in Warfare

A bitter thought is not bitterness. A bitter thought is a bitter thought. When you act on that thought, then it becomes true bitterness.

Just seeing a picture in your mind does not mean that you are in bondage to fear, guilt, or bitterness. It is when you allow it to affect your emotions and then walk it out in your will that it becomes a stronghold.

Yet, satan is such a trickster. Just because you thought it, you think that you have sinned.

"I had a fearful thought. I do not have faith."

"I had a guilty thought. I am lost forever. I have lost my faith, hope, and love. I am going to drown and die."

Jesus said to Peter, "Satan desires to sift you as wheat."

When did Peter sin? Did he sin when he thought about denying Christ or when he opened his big mouth and committed the act of denial? The mind is the battlefield of the enemy, remember?

Just because you thought an angry, fearful, or a guilty thought, that does not mean that you are bound by these things. It means that satan is attacking you!

It means that he is slinging some fiery arrows and boulders at you from his war machine. All you have to do is pick up that shield of faith and hope, and block it.

"I bind that thought right now in Jesus' name. I bind that spirit of strife and vainglory. I bind that anger, hatred, and fear. Satan you will loose your hold. I cast down that imagination, and I bring my thoughts into obedience right now."

STOP BEFORE IT EVOLVES TO SIN

Before it becomes sin, while it is still in the battlefield, before you act out that thought - take it captive, and bring it into obedience. When you do that, you will not walk it out. If you do not walk it out, there is nothing that satan can do to touch you.

When you realize what the enemy is up to, you can grab hold of love once again. He can try and pretend. But, he won't be able to get you to lower your defenses, and you won't get a crack in your wall.

PUT YOUR EYES ON JESUS

Fall in love with Jesus. It will displace the bitterness. Every time you are tempted to get angry, bitter, and frustrated, see Jesus there.

I am going to give you a project that will help you put your eyes back on Jesus. Instead of seeing that person, offense, or anger, see the Lord standing there.

When did the Lord get angry and react like that?

Let that love start coming back. Put your eyes on those around you. Wake up and say, "Jesus, show me that person through your eyes. Let me love them and walk in that love."

You will be so busy loving that love will displace the bitterness. It will be like an antibiotic that goes through your system, purging the effects that the bitterness has had on your life.

Perhaps until now, you have not really had a solution for bitterness, other than to repent. That was a great start. Unfortunately, you repented, but then it came back. So, how do we stop it from coming back? We displace it!

DISPLACING FEAR, GUILT AND BITTERNESS

The Lord said to me once, "When a situation happens where you should feel fear, I want faith to jump out. When you should feel guilt, I want hope to jump out.

When you should feel bitterness, and satan throws that fiery dart at you, I want love to jump out."

I said, "Lord that is a bit far-fetched. I know my flesh. I have lived with it for some years. I battle, and I know it!"

He said, "You do this my way. You submit to me like this - rebuke the devil, and fill your mind with faith, hope, and love. Build the Word into you. See me again and again.

Eventually, that will be your go-to that you reach out for. Instead of reaching out for bitterness, you will reach out for love. Then, when satan comes with his dart, love is going to come out. Hope is going to come out. Faith is going to come out."

The chances are that satan is going to stop throwing those particular fiery darts and find another one because those are not working anymore.

If satan keeps attacking you on the same points again and again, he has found a weak spot in you. Let's take it away from him.

FROM STRONGHOLD TO VICTORY

Proverbs 21:22 says,

> *A wise man attacks the city of the mighty and pulls down the stronghold in which they trust. (NIV)*

Do you want to take the land? Do you want to take his city? You need to start by pulling down the strongholds in your life. Receive a bigger picture. This involves a lot more than you just getting an answer to your prayer.

This involves a lot more than you just taking back your city and your land. This means marching into satan's kingdom and taking back what the enemy has stolen from others.

Start with tearing down these strongholds in your life, and then move to teaching others to tear down these strongholds in theirs.

Deal with your sin. That is the quick part. Then, get healing. That part is also a quick one. God does not waste time.

Then do as Ephesians 6:13 tells you... "having done all – stand." That part takes time. You might have to rebuke the enemy hour after hour if those thoughts keep coming at you.

Cast him down, and change the way that you view this world. Turn that weakness into a strength like Paul said in 2 Corinthians 12:9.

PRACTICAL PROJECTS

I am going to make this a bit easier for you. I have a couple of projects that will help you to do what I have taught. There are three simple projects. You can, and probably will, come back to this chapter again and again.

I have covered a lot of ground. You are going to want to reread these chapters and make more notes.

1. THE CONFESSION SESSION

This will help you to get your eyes back on track again. It will deal with the fear, and it will help you to build your faith again.

It is very simple.

1. Get together with a couple of believers.

It does not matter who. James said, "Confess your sins, one to another." He did not say that you had to confess your sins to your pastor.

If there is another believer, a blood-bought child of God, you can go to them.

2. Have a meeting, and confess your sins to one another. Confess your fears, and have them stand in agreement with you.

Say, "This is what I fear. This is what I feel."

By doing that, you give them license to hold you accountable and make you deal with that fear. While you are still struggling with it in your mind, you are trying to solve the problem yourself, even though you know that you should be bringing this problem to the Lord.

By opening up and confessing to another believer, you make yourself accountable and make them accountable. The prayers of the just avail much! Stand in agreement, and stop trying to fight it in your mind.

Do it as often as you need to do it. This is not a once-off thing. If there are things going wrong in your life, and you are struggling, get together with a group of believers and have a confession session.

Confess your sins one to another. In fact, do not just confess your sins but hold one another accountable to deal with them. That is the secret.

I do not mean for you to say the same as in a Catholic confessional and say, "Father, I have sinned, and I am going to do it again tomorrow."

That is why they do it in a little booth where the "father" cannot see them. I am not subscribing to that. I am subscribing to going to another believer, putting yourself in their hands, and saying, "I am going to confess my sins to you, so that you can help me break free and so that I do not return to that sin again, like a dog to its vomit."

Then, they can confess their sins to me so I will be held accountable for them, and they will be held accountable for me. We will be bearing one another's burdens and are going to see one another through.

That is what it means to be a body. That is what it means to be the family of Christ. We bear one another's burdens.

So, you confess your sins one to another. "This is what I fear. This is what I am guilty about." Just sharing that will set you free.

Having another believer to stand in agreement with you and help you will change everything.

THE PURPOSE OF THE CONFESSION SESSION

This project takes the power of fear away. Half the fear of your fears is that someone is going to find out about your fears.

So, getting it all out, whether someone thinks you are weird or not, will take half the problem away and will make you accountable to deal with that sin.

Then, the power of agreement will keep the enemy at bay. When you are sick, it is hard to have faith for your healing. Get someone else to stand in agreement with you. It will help boost your faith.

It is the same for fear, guilt, and bitterness. Have someone stand in agreement with you.

2. THE BULLDOZING PROJECT

Do you know that a hurricane is formed by a cold and a hot front? As they collide, they start a force of nature that can wreak havoc, tear up whole houses and trees. It destroys everything in its path.

With the bulldozing project, you will start a spiritual hurricane. It is so easy. You take the power of speaking in tongues and the power of quoting the Word, and you start creating a hot and a cold front.

Bulldozing is a simple.

1. Take some of your favorite scriptures that attack the problem at hand, and then quote them for ten minutes.

2. Follow that by speaking in tongues for ten minutes.

3. Switch it, and speak the scriptures again for ten minutes.

4. While doing this, remember to keep your mind focused on the solution to the problem that you are coming against.

What you will have is a cold front and a hot front that will start colliding. You will start feeling it build up inside of you.

It is not good enough just to speak in tongues or just to quote the Word. You have to make sure that you keep focused on the promise that God has given you at all times. Keep that focus, as you are speaking in tongues and feeding the Word into your spirit.

Guess what this does? It gets your mind off your fear, it gets your mind off your bitterness, and it focuses you on what has God said.

Also, by feeding the Word in, you are building up your faith. You are speaking out in tongues, and you are confessing. You are building up your hope because you see the goal in front of you.

As you speak in tongues and see the promise that God has given, you are going to start to feel a bubbling deep inside.

As you are feeding the Word into your mind, guess what you are doing? You are displacing those strongholds. Remember how I shared that satan starts with pictures in your mind?

So, that is how you do it. You speak in tongues, focus on the promise and the goal, and then you speak the Word as you visualize those promises.

"Whoever says to this mountain, be removed..."

You see that mountain being plucked up and removed. Instead of seeing your guilt, shame, or fear, you are seeing that mountain being uprooted. You are seeing the blessing of the Lord that makes one rich.

THE PURPOSE OF BULLDOZING

You are seeing a good outcome painted in the scriptures you are quoting. You are feeding these pictures into your mind. You are renewing your mind with the Word and releasing the power through your spirit in tongues.

When you bring the two together, you have yourself a spiritual hurricane. Good luck to the devil if he is standing in the way because those strongholds are coming down.

You are not just tearing down the strongholds, but you will be displacing the strongholds that the enemy has used to trip you up. You are creating new cities and a stronghold of your own that is going to set him running.

You are going to make that weakness into a strength. You are going to take those negative pictures and displace them with pictures of the Word. Then, you will speak in tongues, according to the will of God and displace all those negative things that you keep saying and seeing.

BUILDING YOUR OWN STRONGHOLDS!

I am going beyond just tearing down the strongholds. I am talking about building a few of your own and making sure that you can take this land that God has given to you.

This is a powerful project that puts your focus on the correct goal. It destroys the work of the enemy. It will increase your faith and change the pictures of your mind.

When that happens, it will change the way you feel. When it changes the way you feel, you will react in faith, hope, and love, instead of in fear and bitterness.

Then, it will be God working with man. That is why bulldozing is such a powerful project. Every Christian should do it. If you are going through spiritual warfare and do not know what is going on, bulldoze until you feel that hurricane.

Bulldoze until you feel a strong force inside of you. Then stand on your land and say, "In the name of Jesus, satan, I tear down every stronghold in my life." Watch things explode and change.

3. THE PRAISE PROJECT

The final project is the praise project. I have already done a full teaching on this, so I am not going to labor the point. But, it is very simple. What are you going through right now? What is your difficulty or hardship? Praise God for it.

You say, "The devil is attacking me."

So what? Why should he get the glory?

"The devil made me sick."

Praise God that you are sick. Why should the devil get the glory? Why should he get my faith, hope, and love? I would rather give it to the Lord.

"Lord, I thank you that I am sick and lying in bed because it gives me the five minutes of peace and quiet that I have not had all year."

Turn around your circumstance, and be grateful for them. Thank the Lord for what you are going through because all things work together for good to those that love the Lord and are called according to His purpose.

Praise puts your eyes on Jesus and restores your love. You cannot sing, worship, thank the Lord, and be grateful for everything, without feeling a force of love bubbling up from deep inside of you.

You feel discouraged, bitter, angry and frustrated at everything that is going on. However, just say, "Thank you Jesus that our bank accounts are empty. Thank you that I am sick and that nobody likes me. Thank you that I am always rejected. Jesus, I praise you for everything that you have given me.

It is because I have been so sad that I realize how happy you make me. It is because I have experienced lack that when you provide, I appreciate it so much."

You only know true joy when you experience sadness. You only understand wisdom when you have been stupid. You only appreciate abundance when you have had a lack.

So, instead of travailing and complaining, why don't you turn around the strongholds that satan has in your life? Take these things that he is attacking you with, and put them into the hands of God.

Start praising Jesus. Start loving Him and thanking Him. Thank Him for the conflict with your spouse.

"Lord, I praise you for the conflict with my spouse. I praise you that we have had problems in our marriage because you can show your glory through it.

I praise you that I am going through this tough time because when I come out on the other side, I am going to stand so strong that satan is never going to get me down again. Thank you, Lord, that you are taking my hand through this and that I am not alone."

You cannot pray that without seeing those pictures, and when you see those pictures, you feel that love. You see Jesus right there, and you are not alone in facing any of those things anymore.

THE PURPOSE OF THE PRAISE PROJECT

This project puts Jesus in control. It takes the enemy's power away. It changes the picture, and it restores your love. Then, instead of always having to have your shield defending against the enemy, you can start throwing a few fiery darts of your own against the enemy.

You can start being strong in your faith, hope, and love and not be moved anymore. When satan comes trying to attack you with his fear - faith will come out and then... he better start running!

You will get stronger, and you will overcome. Then you will have a sword in your hand, and you will help God's people overcome.

So, what's your stronghold? Is it one, two, or all three? Now, you know what to do about it. Pick up that sword in your hand, stand against the enemy, and let us go and take his land together!

SPIRITUAL WARFARE – THE RULES OF ENGAGEMENT

CHAPTER 08 – SPIRITUAL WARFARE – THE RULES OF ENGAGEMENT

A kingdom is defined by a lot more than its city. For years, I have spoken about the Church as a city on a hill. However, as I started looking at the subject of spiritual warfare, I realized that a kingdom is a lot more than just a city.

In fact, I would daresay that the city is the smallest part of a kingdom. Sure, it is the hub. It is where the king resides and where everyone goes to get what they need, whether it is for entertainment or education or to do business.

However, not everyone lives in the city, and most of the work is done outside of the city.

When you look at the city around the time that Jesus walked the earth, you will see that the city may have been the hub. But, it was not the kingdom. David may have lived in Jerusalem and even built it up as a beautiful city on a hill, but his kingdom extended way beyond Jerusalem.

It extended to the surrounding countryside and other smaller cities. This network of cities is what made a kingdom.

I have already taught you how you need to build up the wall of your city. You need to establish that wall strong and thick to ensure that there are no cracks so that the enemy cannot come in.

A STEP OUTSIDE THE WALLS

However, it is not good enough for the Church just to be a city on a hill. If we are going to take the kingdoms of this world for Christ, then we need to step out of our walls. We need to take on the cities of the world, as well as the surrounding landscape, to make all of that part of the kingdom of God.

We are called children of Christ. We are named as ones who belong to the kingdom of God, not just a city. It is good that we build the city strong. In fact, when Ezra and Nehemiah returned to rebuild, the first thing that they rebuilt was the city.

They rebuilt the temple and the walls. They made the city strong because that is the nucleus of a kingdom. Yet, that is not where they lived. They had to go and work the land. They had to go into the surrounding areas and take possession again of the land that God had given them.

That is the sum of what spiritual warfare is about. It is not good enough to take the little bit of land back that you have in this world. If you want to rise up and take back the land for God's people, you have to go beyond your walls.

You have to go beyond your land and take the enemy's cities. That is what defines spiritual warfare.

I ended my teaching on strongholds with the scripture in Proverbs, "If a wise man wants to take a city of a mighty man, he starts with taking down his strongholds."

KNOW YOUR ENEMY

That is where you begin. It is not where you end. If you truly want to take down the city of a mighty man, then you have to go and take down the strongholds of that mighty man. However, how often do you stop at the strongholds?

How often do you stop at the little attacks that satan throws at you? I am going to show you your enemy. I am going to show you how he works and how you can defeat him. I am not going to stop at sharing how to defeat him in your life.

I am talking about going past the plateau. Are you not tired of the plateau in your Christian walk? Are you not tired of the plateau in your finances, relationships, business... and simply every area of your life?

I am talking about taking more and going further than you ever have before. You are not going to do this without engaging in spiritual warfare.

I shared in the message *Hope – The Power of Focus*, how you often make the following mistake: God gives you a promise and you stand in one place waiting for that promise to come to you, instead of realizing that you need to step forward toward the promise.

The same holds true for warfare. You seek the Lord for something that you have never possessed before. You want the fig trees that you did not plant. You want to drink the wine from the vines you did not plant. You want to live in cities that you did not build, just like the Lord told Joshua.

INTO THE LAND BEYOND

You want to experience all these things, but you want to stay at home and do it. There is a reason why you do not have any of those things yet. There is a reason why the righteous have not yet possessed the things of the unjust.

It is because you are not engaging in spiritual warfare and going beyond your comfort zone. You are not going beyond today and tomorrow's problems. You are not going beyond your little needs and stretching yourself further afield to take back the land.

This goes beyond dealing with personal sin. I am talking about engaging in spiritual warfare by picking up your weapons and going into the enemy's camp to take back the things that God wants to give you.

Right now, the enemy is the god of this world. He is the one that has dominion over the systems of this world. It does not mean that it has to stay that way, but right now, that is how it is.

If you want to walk in success, you are going to have to march in and take it. We have to be like John the

Baptist and take it by force. That is what I am going to share with you in this chapter. You need to know your enemy.

How Satan Gains License

Sin

How does satan gain license in your life? I have already shared this in a couple of teachings. Firstly, he gains license through the sin of man, through your sins or the sins of others.

Misguided Prayers

He also gains license through the misguided prayers of believers. You have already learned how powerful your spirit is. You know that when you release what lies in your spirit through words and actions, it has a creative force on this earth.

When you release those words, you create with them. Now, not all the words that you speak create faith, hope, and love. Words do not always create blessings.

If a believer is speaking things that they should not speak and praying things that they should not pray, instead of God working with man, now satan works with man and his creation goes forth.

False Religion

Also, false religions give the enemy power. How many demonic decrees do you find out there? Do you really think that the enemy and his camp are sleeping while the children of God are sleeping?

The enemy has plenty of agents, whether it is through TV, radio, movies or even some standing up behind the pulpit. They are decreeing and speaking forth his will into the earth, instead of God's will.

SATAN WORKING WITH MAN

Every time that happens, satan is given license. Have you ever wondered how attacks can come when you know that you have dealt with your sin, closed all the open doors in your life, and tore down those strongholds?

Circumstances continually come against you. Well, you are not the only one living in this world. Sure, you have the spirit of Christ in you, and your words are more powerful than any unbeliever's words.

However, we are not the only agents in this world. Satan has his agents too, and they are preaching his message every single minute and second of the day.

HOW SATAN CREATES CIRCUMSTANCES

If you go past a mosque, you will hear them praying. What do you think is being released? Satan's will is being released repeatedly on this earth. Since he has that license, he uses it to arrange circumstances in your life to try and get you to give up the land that you have.

Up until now, I have spoken about the warfare that you engage in your own heart, mind, emotions, and will. Yet, from this chapter, I am looking at circumstances that the enemy forms to bring against you. He wants to force you to build strongholds that he can use to rattle you and cause you to open up your city gates.

He will arrange a circumstance in your life that will open up the temptation for you to get bitter and build that foundation again. Because of the license the enemy received from others, he will cause things to bear pressure on you that will tempt you to fear, feel guilty, or become bitter.

He wants you to give in to the lusts of the flesh, and if you do, you build those strongholds. Then he comes closer to home and hits you in your weak spots. When he does that, you end up dropping your guard, and he comes back into your camp.

FACING EXTERNAL DEMONIC ATTACK

You have learned how to deal with the first two types of warfare, but how do you deal with these circumstances? How do you deal with the license that satan has been given out there?

I'll be honest. When you look at the world and all the evil in it, and weigh Christians next to unbelievers and other religions, it can look discouraging. You think, "How are we ever going to overcome?"

You think that you are destined to always be torn down because you are a Christian, and because satan has so much coming against you. Do not forget that the weapons of our warfare are not carnal but mighty in pulling down the strongholds.

The Lord did not lead you this way just so that satan could buffet you continuously. I will go on to explain to you what Jesus meant when He said,

> *John 16:33 These things I have spoken to you, that in Me you may have peace. In the world you will have tribulation; but be of good cheer, I have overcome the world*

Jesus was telling us, "Yes, you will have tribulation in this world. You will have circumstances coming against you. The winds and the waves will hit your boat - but be of good cheer for I have overcome the world!"

If He has overcome the world and is dwelling in me - guess what? You are going to overcome the world! Satan may use his tactics to bring circumstances against us. But not only will we not buckle under those circumstances, we will take them in the palm of our hand and use them as a weapon against him to overcome!

TURNING ATTACKS INTO OPPORTUNITIES

Here is where you will understand that all things work together for good to those that love the Lord and are called according to His purpose. What do you think Romans 8:28 means?

It means that when satan throws a circumstance at you, you do not have to buckle. You can grab that circumstance, turn it around, and use it to give satan an uppercut and so, overcome the world.

You do not just defend or run away and hide. You overcome that circumstance. It serves you. You become the master of your circumstance.

However, you are not going to become the master of your circumstance while you allow the enemy to buckle you and cause you to build his strongholds.

So, let's take hold of our circumstances today and turn them around. Let's make them work for us because that is what God intends.

THREE KINDS OF WARFARE

Satan engages in three kinds of warfare. I have already taught in length on two of those types. So, I will just reiterate a bit here.

1. INSURGENCY WARFARE (GUERILLA WARFARE)

The first kind of warfare that the enemy engages in is insurgency warfare (Guerilla Warfare). This is the kind of warfare where the enemy sneaks in under the cover of night.

He finds a little hole in your wall, and he comes creeping in. It is all about defeating the enemy when he comes against you with this kind of insurgency warfare.

This is about dealing with your generational curses, personal sin, repeated un-repented sin, and the leaven that you pick up from others.

He causes you to fall into sin and listen to the lusts of the flesh. That is all insurgency warfare. He attacks your flesh so that you will sin and not put the sin under the blood. Then... he has you.

He is like a thief in the night coming under the cloak of darkness. He comes into your camp and steals the blessing that God has for you. That is when you see God providing money, and suddenly, satan steals it.

God provides on one hand, - satan steals on the other. God provides you the wife of your dreams, and you end up fighting all the time. Why is this? It is the enemy's insurgency warfare.

2. PSYCHOLOGICAL WARFARE

The second kind of warfare that the enemy uses to attack us is psychological warfare. This is probably the most damaging of all the types of warfare because this is when the enemy attacks your mind, emotions, and will.

This is what I shared in the chapter on Tearing Down Strongholds – Removing Satan's Power. The enemy causes you to build foundations in your life from which he attacks you again and again.

This will cause you to fall into bitterness, fear, and guilt. They cause you to be shaken.

3. OPEN BATTLEFIELD WARFARE

The warfare that I will discuss with you in this chapter is the third kind of warfare, which is open battlefield warfare. It is warfare where you see two enemies lined up, facing each other on the open field, going forward to take the land.

This is the kind of warfare that you can find in the following passages:

John 16:33 says,

> *These things I have spoken to you, that in Me you may have peace. In the world you will have tribulation; but be of good cheer, I have overcome the world.*

It is fascinating to see that Jesus said this before He was crucified. Jesus walked an overcoming walk. No circumstance came against Him that He did not take by the throat to turn around and use to His advantage.

He did not say, "I will overcome the world when I resurrect." He said, "I have overcome the world right now."

We saw how He walked through the crowd that wanted to throw Him over the cliff. We saw Him face the Pharisees that tried to question and trip Him up. We saw when they threw that adulteress woman at His feet and waited for Him to fail.

Every time, satan threw something at Him, whether it was on the pinnacle of the temple as He was being tempted, or the time that they threw that woman at His feet. He took every attack of the enemy and did not only defend Himself, but He turned each circumstance around and used that to take ground.

USING CIRCUMSTANCES TO YOUR ADVANTAGE

Is that not what happened with Lazarus? Everyone said, "If only you would have come sooner, Lord." There was the death of the one He loved so much and everyone was saying, "He could do so much for everyone else, but He cannot do anything for the one He loves." Satan threw those barbs at Him.

You get these attacks in life that make you look like a fool, and you think, "What am I going to say? I failed, and now they are calling me on it."

However, Jesus did not allow them to call Him on it. He stood boldly, and in a loud voice said, "Lazarus, come forth!" He took that circumstance, and He turned it around. That is your model - to not buckle under circumstances, but to use them to your advantage.

That is the core of true spiritual warfare.

THE SYSTEMS OF THE WORLD

CHAPTER 09 — THE SYSTEMS OF THE WORLD

1 Thessalonians 5:5

> *You are all sons of light and sons of the day. We are not of the night nor of darkness.*

As I came to prepare this teaching, the Lord said, "The world is in travail between light and darkness, good and evil." We cannot do this the world's way. We have to do this God's way. We have to be children of the light.

This means that we cannot compromise and be of this world. We must stand in His power and take this world for Christ.

1 Corinthians 2:12 says,

> *Now we have received, not the spirit of the world, but the Spirit who is from God, that we might know the things that have been freely given to us by God.*

Satan is going to use the systems of this world to create circumstances to get you down.

THE SYSTEMS OF THE WORLD

In the systems of the world, he has all the people that he needs at his disposal. He has all the agendas, power, and license that he needs. So, he will use the systems to bear those terrible circumstances on you to cause you to build strongholds and open the gates of your city.

Since I knew this fact my whole life, I always thought the systems were bad. I said, "The systems of the world are evil. The rich of this world are satan incarnate."

This is nothing new. It is a doctrine that is taught in the Church. We had some teaching that said, "If you go to the doctor, you are going to the devil. The medical system is a system of the world, which is satan's throne room. If you go to the doctor, you are bowing down to satan."

We had Christians in the past that did not want to watch TV or listen to the radio because it was the devil's system.

This is a doctrine that has been bred into us, especially for those of us that have grown up through, and have parents that were involved in, the Pentecostal revival. That teaching has been put into us again and again.

SYSTEMS VS. SPIRIT OF THE WORLD

The Lord blew my mind as I prepared this teaching. He said to me, "The systems are not evil. The spirit of the world is evil. The systems of this world were created by man."

I was reminded of Genesis where the Word tells us that we were created by God. Whether you are a believer or an unbeliever, you were created in the image of God. This means that you have a piece of His wisdom inside of you.

As believers, God brings His Holy Spirit and renews our spirit, and so, we have so much more than unbelievers do. However, even in this world, an unbeliever still has more power than a dog. Why? It is because they have a spirit.

The Lord said to me, "I put a spirit of creativity in man. Look around you. Look at the things that man has created."

I love my iPad. Guess what? That was created by a man. Thank the Lord for the internet. Man created that too.

The Lord said to me, "Man created the systems of this world. The systems are not wrong. The spirit of the one who created it is wrong."

That is why the Lord tells us not to love the world. We are to love Him so that we have His Spirit, and then we can influence the systems of this world.

However, what have you done? You are sitting in your city on a hill instead of going out there and taking this land for Christ. You are happy with your little portion at the bottom of the rung, instead of remembering that you are the head and not the tail, above and not beneath.

GOD WANTS TO USE THE SYSTEMS

You do not have to take second best in this world. You can be like Israel and march into the Promised Land to take hold of the kingdoms of this world.

In the times of Solomon, because he brought so much blessing, he brought blessing to all the nations that surrounded him too. He brought blessing by trading with foreign nations.

He was not just a blessing for himself. He was a blessing to others. He instituted systems, cities, and entire lands that blessed more than just the children of Israel.

Your thinking is too small. You have to go beyond. You have to stop fighting the system and start binding the enemy. The spirit of the world is what you need to wage warfare against.

Here is a newsflash - God wants to use the systems of this world to bless His people.

How else do you think the money is going to come? Where do you think the blessing, the property, whatever you need to do the work that God has called you to do, is going to come from?

Do you think it is going to drop out of the sky? If He is going to give you money, there is going to be currency involved. It is going to have to come through a bank account or a business transaction. Something needs to happen.

I am not saying that God cannot rain money from the sky. He put a gold coin in the mouth of a fish. However, that gold coin was man made. It came from somewhere, and people recognized it as a currency they knew. Otherwise, you could not pay with it.

God used the world back then to bless His people. He put Adam and Eve in the Garden of Eden, and He did not drop fruit from heaven. The fruit came from the trees, which fed off the soil, which fed off the water in the ground.

If God is going to bless you, He is going to bless you through this world. However, you need to go and take hold of that blessing. Eve did not sit down and say, "Apple, come to me." She had to walk up to the tree, pick the apple, and eat the apple.

GOD WORKING WITH MAN

We have to do our part. God has done His part. When I realized that, I suddenly understood this passage:

Romans 13:1-2 says,

> *Let every soul be subject to the governing authorities. For there is no authority except from God, and the authorities that exist are appointed by God.*
> *2 Therefore whoever resists the authority resists*

*the ordinance of God, and those who resist will
bring judgment on themselves.*

I did not like this scripture in times past because there
were certain authorities that really were not godly.
However, this scripture is saying that God gave some of
His authority to man on this earth.

Whether saved or unsaved, He has given man authority
in this earth. This earth belongs to man. He has given
us the right to name the animals, to take the clay in the
ground and to build skyscrapers with it.

You can take the diamonds that come from coal and
decorate yourself with them. He has given that license
to man. He gave man license to set up governing
authorities for himself. He gave us the license to rule
ourselves.

GOD - THE FINAL AUTHORITY

That is part of His grace, and it is a doctrine all on its
own. I am not going to go into the doctrine of the grace
of God. However, the point is that these systems, and
even the authorities, essentially come from God
because God gave some authority to man. Then man
gave authority to another man, which was given to
another man....

When we vote and put someone in authority over us,
we hand our authority over to that person. That is why,
ultimately, the final authority is God's. Do you
understand?

If you get the picture that man is the one who set up the systems of this world, the following scripture comes to life.

1 John 4:4 says,

> *You are of God, little children, and have overcome them, because He who is in you is greater than he who is in the world.*

It does not say that you just defeat them or back down from them. I love this word "overcome."

When you look at the systems of this world - it feels overwhelming. You think, "Lord, how can the righteous become rich in such a sinful world? When a righteous person does rise up, there are many that oppose them all the time."

This is true, but I am reminded of the history of the children of Israel. All of the gentiles were sinning. They were sacrificing idols and bowing down to gods that they should not bow down to. They were even giving their children over to the sacrifice of Moloch and of Baal. They were choosing their own road.

STAND IN AUTHORITY

They had their systems established and their structure all set up. They were going the way that they wanted to go. Yet, it only took the work of some prophets to walk amongst those systems and declare the will of God.

The word that the prophets spoke tore down the temples and cities. It also changed the course of entire nations - making the systems that man made bow to the word of God. Israel indeed got to live in cities that they did not build!

How much authority do you need to change your circumstances and the systems of this world? You do not need a whole lot because you can send a thousand to flight all by yourself.

So, if just one of those prophets could speak words that came to pass, that created the circumstances, how much more do you have today being a blood-bought child of God with the indwelling of the Holy Spirit?

You have authority to speak forth, create, and cause the systems of this world to come into line with the Word of God and therefore create circumstances that are favorable to God's people.

Jeremiah 25:9 says,

> *Behold, I will send and take all the families of the north,' says the Lord, "and Nebuchadnezzar the king of Babylon, My servant, and will bring them against this land, against its inhabitants, and against these nations all around, and will utterly destroy them, and make them an astonishment, a hissing, and perpetual desolations.*

This guy killed men, women, and children. He worshiped other idols. He tore down the temple, went into the most sacred place, and destroyed everything that belonged to God. Yet, God calls him His servant.

Here is the revelation. God uses the system for His own means.

Stop attacking the system. It is a fight between light and darkness. Our voice needs to be heard more than the spirit of the world so that God can use those systems to our advantage.

USING THE SYSTEMS TO GOD'S ADVANTAGE

When the word of God proceeds out of the mouth of one standing in prophetic office, the "Nebuchadnezzars" and "Pharaohs" out there basically become servants in the hand of God.

When those decrees have gone forth, God will use the very impulses of the world to steer those "servants" in a direction that blesses the Church.

Do you understand this logic? When I saw this, my spirit exploded. Instead of travailing about how evil the world is, perhaps we should start putting our faith in God who is able to use that evil, and steer it in a direction that brings blessing to us.

All things work together for good for those who love the Lord. How else do you think the wealth of the unjust is going to become the wealth of the just? The unjust need to make some mistakes, and I know just the person who knows their weakness!

I have seen this myself so many times. When we first moved to Mexico, we were paying a fortune to get online and preach the word of God. We were paying $1,000 a month for a telephone bill.

However, we paid it because we needed to be online. It was our lifeline. It was the avenue that God used at that time for us to reach people.

We did not have that money, so we got down on our knees and prayed and prayed. You will not believe what happened. God did not give us $1,000 for the bill. Do you know what He did do?

Overnight, the telephone system of the region that we were staying in changed dramatically. They made internet unlimited for a lower fee than most countries would pay!

Instead of paying $1,000 a month, it went down to $50 a month for unlimited internet access. That is what I am talking about. Why are we not sending out these kinds of prayers?

However, we are sitting around praying for $1,000. Why do we not just pray that God will use the systems of this world, even in their evil, to bless His people? That is warfare. That is open warfare. That is how we are going to take the land back.

NAMING THE SYSTEMS OF THE WORLD

CHAPTER 10 – NAMING THE SYSTEMS OF THE WORLD

Ephesians 2:2 says,

> *In which you once walked according to the course of this world, according to the prince of the power of the air, the spirit who now works in the sons of disobedience.*

We know that the spirit that now works in us is the Holy Spirit, who teaches us all things. So, we see a comparison again between light and darkness. They are called children of disobedience. They walk after the course of this world.

In other words, they followed their flesh. They were of the world. They did things the world's way - the status quo way.

Yet, we are not of this world. We are of the Holy Spirit, and we are going to create our own systems in this world so that the children of disobedience get to do things our way.

That is warfare. That is what it means to take ground. The Lord gave me seven main systems of this world.

As I name these systems, you are going to see where your circumstantial attacks are coming from. You are going to see where you have been experiencing people, circumstances and pressure bearing down on you through these systems.

1. RELIGIOUS SYSTEM

In the religious system, we are forced to recognize all religions. We are not allowed to "rock the boat." Christians have to stand up and say, "Homosexuality is ok. It is the way that you were born."

We are not allowed to call it sin anymore. We are not allowed to stand on our own convictions and have our own views and beliefs, and be loud and proud about them. We are not allowed to pray at school.

Why not? We are not allowed because of the religious system. First, you get so discouraged. You think, "The world is going into darkness and destroying everything."

However, it is interesting because the world hangs itself by its own rope. Since the world has given such freedom of religion to every religion, they cannot in the next breath take away the freedom of Christianity either, without taking away the freedoms of every other religion.

So, what started out as a system of this world where satan thought that he would take away our freedom, became a system where he actually gave us more of it. I can tell you right now, that if anyone tries to come against me, I just need to stand up and say, "I am sorry, but that goes against my beliefs."

That is a lovely buzzword, isn't it? It works for every other religion out there, and it now works for Christianity even more.

ARISE AND SHINE!

Satan thought that he would bring all these false religions in and make us lose hope, and that is exactly what the Church did. The Church lost hope.

We say, "There are so many Muslims, Jehovah Witnesses, and Mormons." What are you going to do about it? We start diminishing the power of God to change this system, instead of realizing that God is allowing a deep darkness to cover the earth and the people, so that He may arise and shine and kings may be drawn to the brightness of His rising. (Isaiah 60)

The darkness will be so dark in the religious system that through that darkness, Christianity will be able to rise up as a beacon of hope. However, we are so busy competing instead of shining.

You should do what Ephesians 6:13 instructs - after doing all you can, you should stand. You need to stand in boldness, using the systems of this world. If they are going to give something to one religion, then they are giving it to me too.

I am going to take those things. And, where one religion could only do so much with their freedom, we can take that little loophole and blow it out of proportion with the power of God. All we need is a little bit of wisdom and obedience.

This is what God is raising up His Joshuas to do. He is calling them to go into the land to conquer and divide it. He is raising up those in the religious system that will do just that.

It is not going to happen by us comparing ourselves to others. It is going to happen by us shining brighter, being bolder, and being more confident and unashamed of who we are.

PROUDLY UNASHAMED

If Wicca and Jehovah's Witnesses can be unashamed, why can't we be doubly unashamed? Yet, we are too busy complaining about how bad the world is that we do not stop to shine that light that we have and take the land that God has given to us.

People are not going to be drawn to our nattering and complaining. The Word does not say, "Arise, shine, for your nattering and complaining has come."

I keep hearing Christians complaining about how bad things are. What are you going to do about it? Arise, shine, for your light has come!

Let us shine! Let us be bright! Let us be bold! Let us be full of fire, and let them come and watch us burn. Now, we are using the religious system to our advantage.

2. EDUCATIONAL SYSTEM

Next is the educational system that goes from primary school to Bible college and university. This is satan's pulpit where he gets to spread his doctrine.

I remember one of the first conflicts that we had in ministry. Someone said to my father, "Since you are homeschooling your children, what history are you going to teach them?"

My father, ever the prophet, said, "Why should I teach them history? It just indoctrinates them according to the archetype of that country."

People are always saying that you have to teach your children about freedoms and this and that... but why? Would you not rather teach them about the kingdom of God?

You would not believe how much opposition comes when you start challenging the educational system.

"Are your kids going to college?"

"Why should they?"

"Because that is what everyone else does."

What if God does not want them to? What if God has a different road for them to take? I am not saying that education is bad. I am saying that the spirit is bad. I am saying that the pressure that is put on us to conform is bad.

Before you think that all is lost, I will let you know that God has an upper hand. Satan thought that he would quench our fire in the schools. He thought that he would take prayer out of the schools and start preaching evolution, under the name of "broadening your horizons" and "reaching higher wisdom."

CHRISTIANS BIRTH HOMESCHOOLING

First, it seemed as if God was ripped out of the educational system. Then, homeschooling was born. Guess who spearheaded the homeschooling system that is now rampant all over the world?

Christians spearheaded the homeschooling movement. God raised up for Himself a couple of Daniels and Solomons that said, "Education is not bad. We need to teach ourselves Mathematics, English, Biology, and Science. We need to have the knowledge of this world, but we do not need to have the wisdom of this world."

What we need is the knowledge of this world and the wisdom of God so that we can walk in wisdom.

That is why when you look at home schooling and the materials, you will see a different doctrine being taught. You will find very little on evolution and all the things that tear down the things that we believe.

Everyone complained about how bad the schools were getting, but it gave birth to a movement that is changing the course of our education right here and now. It is giving us something new, and those who are on the forefront of it, who had the confidence to stand up and be different, are now recognized by the world.

What started out as a "Christian only" thing has now become very widespread because darkness started covering the earth and it became more and more dangerous to send your children to school.

The darkness descended in such a thick cloud that even the world could not stand the darkness. They became like the Egyptians that went with the Israelites to the Promised Land.

They had a mixed multitude because the people thought that it was too dark there for them, and they saw a ray of hope. Here is a place where children can get a proper education, and you do not have to fear for their lives.

So where did these people go? They went to all the Christian homeschool systems. Do you know what we can have in there? We can have the spirit of Christ in there. We do not have to be arrogant. We can just stand and be bold.

So, before you think that the systems of this world are lost to us, start realizing that they are tools for us to take this land more than ever before.

3. FINANCIAL SYSTEM

Next we have the financial system, from banking to taxes. All you need to do is get a parking ticket, and you will feel the financial system bearing down on you. You have that pressure, through levies and taxes, like the guys that went to Peter and said, "Does your master pay the temple tax?"

He said, "Of course he pays the temple tax."

Later on the religious leaders came to Jesus and said, "Should we pay taxes or not?"

Jesus said, "Give to Caesar what is Caesar's and to God what is God's."

JOSEPH TAKING HIS PLACE

Before you start moaning about the financial system, realize that God is raising up Josephs. Do you know what Joseph did? He taxed the people.

He sold the grain of Egypt back to the people who filled the silos with that grain. Then, when they ran out of money, they sold him their lands, cattle, and themselves.

Then, he levied a whole new tax saying, "Everything you have belongs to Pharaoh now. So, we are going to give you the grain and the land back, but here is a huge tax that you are going to pay."

After that, he took all that money and used it to bless his own people with it. He gave them a land that they did not have to pay tax for and gave them grain that they did not have to pay for.

FIND THE LOOPHOLE

He found a loophole. He used his position and the blessing that God bestowed upon him to bring blessing to his people. Even now, God is raising up those Josephs in this financial institute that we hate so much, to bring blessing and to bring a reprieve to God's people.

Instead of complaining about how difficult the government is, perhaps we should be praying that God puts some Josephs on the throne. So then we can, as believers, walk in the blessing that God has for us.

We are so busy speaking curses. Are we so surprised that things are not getting better? Why can't the government suddenly give a tax break to believers? Why can't the government turn things in our favor? Why not?

You have been thinking too small.

4. POLITICAL SYSTEM

Then, you have the political system where you have all these parties vying for power. Come election time, there is a whole song and dance with people tearing each other down to see who's better and who can bring out the most "dirty laundry."

Everyone puts their faith in man, instead of God. There are two extremes. There are those that think that they need to be like the world with a Christian message and those that believe that they should not touch politics at all.

ENTER: MORDECAI AND ESTHER

Yet, God is raising up His Mordecais and Esthers who will be set apart but influential in the laws that will govern the land. These are the systems of man, and we need to have a say in the systems of man.

Until we pray and release and do our part, we are not going to change these systems. That is where our warfare is coming from. This political system gives pressure to conform to national beliefs.

Having traveled so much, if there is one political system that we have personally faced again and again, it has to be the immigration system.

GOD BENDS THE SYSTEM IN OUR FAVOR

Being from South Africa, going to Mexico, to the United States, to Europe, and all over the place, we always hit this terrible pothole with visas and paperwork. It is such a struggle and travail.

Even in Mexico, it cost us so much money. We got in on a visa that we had to renew every year. It was a lot of money, a lot of stress, and we had to organize piles of paperwork. We had to pay per member in the household.

It was a whole thing just to maintain our residence and stay in the country. We started praying for favor and saying, "Lord, there has to be a better way."

It felt like overnight the Mexican government changed their entire immigration policy. This meant that certain new visas would come out, and it looked good. However, with the changes, it meant that the restrictions were much higher than before.

It did not look like a blessing at first, until we went into the office for our yearly renewal. Whoever handled our paper looked at it and bumped us up to a permanent visa that we never had to renew again. This happened without us having to do anything.

Not only did we not have to supply as much paperwork, but now we never had to renew our visas ever again.

God used that transition and put us at the right place at the right time and in the hand of the right person so that we got unprecedented favor.

That is how God uses the system. It opened a door for us to move freely and not be restricted when doing His work. Stop fighting the system. Start praying for God to use the system to your advantage, and then you will start seeing change in this world.

5. ENTERTAINMENT SYSTEM

Then, we have the entertainment system. I do not need to go deeply into this topic. We have movies, music, and all of the arts, speaking forth the enemy's message and changing the way that we think.

These things are conforming our minds to the spirit of this world. With every movie you watch, guess how much slang you pick up and start using? Guess how many phrases you use?

How many opinions do you have that are satan's doctrine? These things come from the entertainment world. This is such a huge stronghold. It is one of the strongest strongholds the enemy has in this world.

ENTER: DAVID

God is raising up His Davids right now. I see more Christian movies than ever before. Yes, we have some super weird movies coming out about the Bible that are not so Christian at all...including ones made by unbelievers.

At first, you could get a little angry at the misuse of the Scripture, but I am thinking to myself, "Are the Christians such a force to be reckoned with that unbelievers are seeing us as an untapped market? Is the world trying to appease us by creating Christian or Bible-based movies to get our attention?"

Do you know what I see? I see the world trying to make us happy. I see the world trying to get our dollar and our butts into their movie theaters. Guess what that makes us? It makes us above and not beneath, the head and not the tail.

The spirit in those movies is terrible, and there is hardly any God in there at all. They have a messed up view of who God is. Yet, it makes me realize that even the entertainment world is waking up to a whole new dimension that they have not touched before.

Why did this happen? It happened because some select believers with a passion for moviemaking, and a passion for the arts, started shining brightly with all the fire that was in them. They are saying, "Look at us."

People that did not even have the support of those around them had the confidence to stand up, and they made an impact. They started making waves, and those waves got attention.

Just like with homeschooling, we are going to see Christians starting to create a system in the entertainment world. Soon there will be an entire Christian genre of entertainment because we are making waves. We are not being quiet anymore.

We are displacing the systems of this world. Let's not tear the systems down. Let's displace them from the inside out. That is real warfare.

6. MEDICAL SYSTEM

Now, let's move on to the medical system. I remember when my father was diagnosed with diabetes. We went from doctor to doctor, and all they had to give was bad news. The way they spoke, you would think that he was going to drop dead in five minutes.

They would say, "That is bad, but it could be worse because you could die of a heart attack. You better be careful."

ENTER: SAMSON

They preach their doctrine of fear so that you will open that stronghold of fear and allow satan to attack you again and again. However, God is raising up His Samsons, and even though they have been under attack, they will take down the enemy in their very house.

He is also raising up the Aarons that will set up the structure and teach God's people the truth. They will walk them through healing and give them the anointing oil that they need to break free and tear down that fear.

BRINGING THE RIGHT BALANCE

The medical system is a bit of a tricky one, especially if you look at it from the perspective of the Pentecostal revival. They said that the medical system is from the devil. Yet, I see Luke, who was a doctor, being used of God on his travels with Paul.

Then, I read of Paul saying, "This brother of ours got so sick, we feared he was going to die." You would think that God always just healed people. However, God did not always just heal. Sometimes they had to travail through.

Sometimes, they needed a little bit of oil and prayer. You look at the story of the water that flows from the temple and goes out into the land, and it said, "Next to the river were trees for healing."

The trees were for healing the nations. It was always in God's plan for us to receive healing. I see, even in this, Christians rising up and saying, "There has to be a better way. Yes, you trust God for your healing, but what if you just took care of the body that God gave you?"

I spoke about this in the message, *The Tree of Life*. I spoke about tapping into your spirit to heal your body, but how about doing things naturally? How about eating right and taking care of your body?

There I am seeing a whole thrust of medicine that is not medicine at all, but is still rocking the boat. You do not have to be on insulin for the rest of your life. Maybe you can just eat properly and take care of yourself.

You do not have to be on medication for the rest of your life. You do not have to be sick or suffer. You can take of the blessing that God has already put in this land, and take care of your body.

Is that not what medicine is? Does it not give your body the opportunity to heal itself?

So, even in this medical world, there are those who say, "There has got to be a better way. We have to change the way things are."

So, do not knock this. Ask God what part He needs you to play in it. Even in the Old Testament, you will see how the priests had to take care of the medical needs. In fact, look through the law sometime and see how much they had to do in regards to their health, well-being, and cleanliness.

God set the standard for the medical industry way back then. So it is about time that we take hold of it and make it our own once again. We need to lead God's people in a balanced way, using the Spirit and the wisdom of God so that they can break free.

7. COMMERCIAL SYSTEM – MARKETPLACE

Finally, we have the commercial system. This is your career, or your job. If you want to make money in today's world, you have to do it the world's way. That is how the doctrine goes.

However, God is raising up His Moses' right now who are leading the children of God out of that bondage and into the Promised Land. They are learning to do business God's way. They are learning to rise up and make money in this world, God's way.

If you try to do it the world's way, they are going to squash you. What if we did something outside of the box? What if we started businesses that are outside of the box, in a realm where satan has not set up a system yet?

That is what God wants us to do. He wants us to get wisdom, and He wants us to start businesses and establish organizations where we are bringing in money from the unjust to the just.

I would dare say that this is the main way that God is going to bring money in from the world to the Church. It will be through business. It is not going to drop out of the sky. Unbelievers are not going to come to church and say, "Here is our money. We are going to starve. You are welcome to it."

We need to have better businesses, better business ideas, and be on the cutting edge of what God wants to do in the commercial system.

This system is one that is exploding in the Church right now. I am seeing God raise up leaders in commerce everywhere. They are saying, "We can use the system of the world to bring in the money for the Church, instead of just depending on the pittance that we get."

We can walk in the wisdom of Solomon! Gone is the idea that if you just pray enough, someone will put money into your bank account. Now it is a case of sending out the decrees and standing in faith for the system to come in line with the Word of God!

It is time to pray that the trends and changes in the commercial world give the church an advantage. There are many that are torn between this passion and their ministry call, not realizing that they are one and the same.

We cannot rely any longer on the preaching of tithing if we are to make the Church a city on a hill. It is going to take a lot more than a few "cheerful givers" to propel the Church to where it needs to go.

No, we need the Solomons to rise up and take their place. We need them to walk out the wisdom that God has for us - the kind of wisdom that had Jacob putting up sticks in front of the cattle when they mated.

Crazy wisdom that had Joshua walking around the walls of Jericho and Peter throwing out his net "on the other side" after a night of failure. The Word is full of financial wisdom, because God intends to steer this system to our advantage. The key being that we do it His way and with His spirit.

A RECAP OF THE SYSTEMS

These are what these systems look like. When you look at these seven systems, you understand where your attacks have been coming from.

You have the religious system where you stand up and preach a message, and everyone opposes you. It creates a circumstance where you are rejected.

You have your educational system where God says, "I do not want you to go to university. I want you to drop your studies and go into the mission field." You feel the pressure, and it creates a circumstance.

Then, you have your financial system - you have the taxes and traffic tickets. You also have your political system with laws that hinder us from doing what we feel that God needs us to do.

You have the entertainment system where you have believers listening to worldly music. They think that it is cool. It is not cool.

Then comes the medical system bearing pressure saying, "You cannot have the flu without needing us for flu shots." When you do not do it, you rock the boat.

Lastly, you have the marketplace, the commercial system where we are trying our best to make ends meet.

Victory is ours, but first, we need to put the power of God in our mouths and work these systems to our advantage.

CHAPTER 11

RULES OF ENGAGEMENT

CHAPTER 11 — RULES OF ENGAGEMENT

The rules of engagement are simple. There are three of them.

1. THE WALLS - INSURGENCE WARFARE

Firstly, you need to counteract that insurgency warfare. You do that by closing up the walls.

> *1 Peter 4:17 For the time [is come] that judgment must begin at the house of God: and if [it] first [begin] at us, what shall the end [be] of them that obey not the gospel of God? (KJV)*

This means that you seek your heart first. When you have a circumstance coming against you, when you are under pressure from any one of these systems, step one is to check out those walls. Start the judgment with yourself.

"Father, if I opened the door to sin in any way…"

The first rule of engagement is to search your own heart and look for any leaven that you have allowed to get into your lump. Look for any sin that you did not repent of, a generational curse, or a repeated un-repented sin.

That should not take you long, especially if you have already worked through the other teachings that I shared with you.

2. THE STRONGHOLDS — PSYCHOLOGICAL WARFARE

This is when you start dealing with the strongholds - the psychological warfare. You tear down those strongholds of fear, guilt, and bitterness. As those attacks keep coming into your mind, stand against the enemy, rebuke them, and get healing for all your templates.

3. THE BATTLEFIELD — OPEN WARFARE

This is the one we are doing now - open warfare.

1 Chronicles 18:1 says,

> *After this it came to pass that David attacked the Philistines, subdued them, and took Gath and its towns from the hand of the Philistines.*

Here we read about all the nations that were defeated. It speaks about how David defeated this guy and the next. There was a whole lot of smiting going on.

In this chapter you find a list of all the lands that he took. However, he did not stop there.

1 Chronicles 25:1 says,

> *Moreover David and the captains of the army separated for the service some of the sons of Asaph, of Heman, and of Jeduthun, who should prophesy with harps, stringed instruments, and cymbals. And the number of the skilled men performing their service was*

He did not just take the land - he put something else in its place. He set up these guys to prophesy twenty-four hours a day, to bring about the change and maintain his kingdom. Therein is the secret of what we need to do.

OPEN WARFARE 101

If you want to start removing satan's license, the first thing that you need to do is to bind the princes (1 Corinthians 2:6).

1. BIND THE PRINCES

You need to deal with the princes of these systems because you can be sure that satan has a few of them.

Satan has his princes declaring his will. Those princes have been given license by those in the world that are blaring satan's message. The more power he gets, the bigger his prince is.

He has princes over countries, cities, and over systems, and they gain their authority through the words spoken through satan's agents. (Ephesians 6:12)

So, let's change the dynamic, shall we?

You can counteract that. One prophet can change the course of a nation. Why can't one believer change the course of a system if he prayed in faith? Why can't he remove that mountain and cast it into the sea?

2. REMOVING SATAN'S AUTHORITY

You start by binding and renouncing the hold that satan has.

"In the name of Jesus, I take authority over you - you prince of darkness. I do not care who has given you license. You - prince over the financial system that has been manipulating it to your own ends, I take away your authority, and I cause you to come under my feet now, in Jesus' name."

However, don't stop there. It is not enough to take the land or bind the enemy. You must put something in its place.

3. GIVE GOD LICENSE

Luke 11 speaks about the man who was demonized and the demons were cast out of him. It goes on to say that if nothing else were put back, those demons would come back and find a clean home. That man would be in a worse state than he was in before.

The solution is to put something in the demon's place... the Holy Spirit! How much warfare do we do tearing down the kingdom of darkness and then, for five minutes, you feel a release, only to wake up tomorrow and find the enemy staring you in the face again?

What did you put in his place? Yes, you need to go tear down the princes of darkness. You must give God license and decree God's word continuously.

It comes back to that bulldozing project that I gave you. It will certainly give you that authority. I certainly do not mean just speaking the Word. I mean speaking decrees and being on the front line.

USE THE POWER OF DECREE

The power of decree gives God license, and then God can put His angels and archangels in place to change that system. That is real spiritual warfare. You dethrone the enemy and then give God the throne.

It is not about personal sin, inner healing, or dealing with your heart anymore. You dealt with that already. You took five minutes to deal with that. This warfare that you engage in is going to be the bulk of your warfare.

The other stuff is an ongoing habit that you should do when you feel yourself fall. In that case, get it under the blood, then get up, and move on. However, it is in open warfare where you take the enemy's cities and make his kingdom ours.

THE ROLE OF THE FIVEFOLD MINISTRY

This battle line, being in the forefront, is where you are going to find the fivefold ministry. If you have been called to one of the fivefold ministries, you are going to be very familiar with this battle line.

Yes, every believer can do this kind of warfare, but it is the fivefold ministry that will do it with war machines of their own.

THE EVANGELISTS

The evangelist is the one that is going to give conviction of sin so that we can patch up those walls and identify where those cracks are. He is going to call forth conviction to God's people.

He removes satan's hold in their lives and speaks forth decrees of conviction. He cries out for whole nations, "Give me this nation Father!"

He is going to cry out to God, declare, and say, "Satan, give up that country. That country is mine! It belongs to God. You, prince of Switzerland, prince of America, prince of Mexico, you are coming down! Those people belong to God. I speak forth the revival power right now in Jesus' name."

That is the evangelist! He is on the front line waving his banner high and calling those kingdoms to come into subjection.

It is great to lead people to the Lord, but the evangelist does not start there. The evangelist starts on the battlefield - win their hearts in the spirit, and then they can win their hearts in the natural.

THE PASTORS

They are the guys who are going to help God's people overcome that psychological warfare. As the enemy comes against them with those sticks and stones to try to get them to buckle, it is the pastor that is going to pick them up to stand again.

He is going to take them through the inner healing and lead them to still waters. He is also the one that is going to pick up the shepherd's staff, sling, and the stones to attack the lion and the bear to protect God's people.

When the enemy comes like a roaring lion with circumstances against God's people, it is the pastor that is going to stand up and say, "In the name of Jesus, I come against this spirit of strife in marriages in the church. I bind every demon of addiction in the church."

The pastor is a lot more than one who stands up and gives a good preach. He is someone who stands up and makes himself accountable for the sins of God's people. He makes sure that they are defended from the bear and the roaring lion that comes to steal, kill, and destroy.

That is the pastor on the front line, tearing down the attacks on families, businesses, and relationships. The pastor is the one who is going to speak the protection of God over His people, over their hearts and over their minds.

THE TEACHERS

Then, the teachers are going to renew the minds of God's people. If you speak to a teacher, you will find that they can be very sensible until it comes to the subject of heresy.

A true teacher of God gets angry at heresy being taught in the church. If you want to get him on his soapbox, tell him that someone taught something that is contrary to the Word of God.

You are going to see those teachers standing out there, in fire, tearing down that educational system saying, "That is a lie from the pit of hell. Here is the truth.

I bind every lie that has come through colleges and all other schools. I speak forth the renewed mind of Christ. I speak forth those that are going to rise up and teach the truth and lead your people to truth."

That is what the teacher in office looks like on the front lines. Every single one of them needs to engage in spiritual warfare if they are going to reach the hearts and minds of God's people. They need to engage in spiritual warfare first, so that the way is prepared.

This kind of warfare prepares the minds of God's people to receive the truth and so be set free indeed. The teacher is one that will pray for the light in this passage:

> *2 Corinthians 4:6 For it is the God who commanded light to shine out of darkness, who*

has shone in our hearts to give the light of the knowledge of the glory of God in the face of Jesus Christ.

THE PROPHETS

Then, we have the prophets. These are the guys that will speak forth the decrees. They will say, "Satan, you know that land that you thought was yours? Open up, I am coming in. Hand over your keys, devil."

They are the ones who will birth and decree – causing things in heaven to be brought to earth. They will open doors that have been shut, uproot the things that have been planted, put things in place, and decree governments to rise up or be torn down.

They will decree God's will into this earth. That is why the prophet and the apostle work so closely together. It is because before the apostle can start to build, the prophet has to clear the land. They have to come with a spiritual bulldozer and tear down those systems.

They have to tear down the foundations of the enemy so that a new foundation can be built. That is why the power of a prophet is in their mouth and why they are used so much of God in intercession. They are not just used in the lives of God's people, but to speak forth and tear down those strongholds.

I have done a whole teaching on the prophet's role in warfare, so I won't labor the point here.

THE APOSTLES

Finally, we have the apostles, and they do the final stage of warfare, which is to displace and rebuild. Do you remember that the systems were built by man? So then, why don't we just rebuild them?

It will take an apostle to rebuild because he has to get a pattern from the Lord. It cannot be the spirit of this world. It has to be the spirit of God. He cannot be born of this world. He has to be born of the spirit.

This means that not only does he need to be anointed by God, but he needs to have a revelation of the pattern that he needs to build because whatever he builds will be like Solomon.

Not only will that which he builds influence the Church, but it will influence the world as well. I am going to cut this short, because in the chapters that follow, I am going to look at this more.

THE SECRET TO MAINTAINING VICTORY

That is how we are going to maintain the victory. This leads to the final step. The ultimate warfare after this, to maintain our land and make sure that it stays in our hand, is to rebuild.

The displacement of the system is our ultimate goal, just like Solomon who went out and rebuilt the cities of the lands that David conquered. However, you cannot rebuild if you do not take the land first.

You want God to give you wisdom on how to do business, and on all these systems, but you have not yet done the spiritual warfare to take the land. How can you build if you have not taken the land?

That is why this is all about being in the open battle. It is time that we pick up our swords. I do not know about you, but as soon as I am done writing this chapter, I will be standing on my land afresh.

I will say, "You, princes of the air that have been given license to bring circumstances against me, I bind you right now in the name of Jesus."

Then, I will decree God's plan for my life, my ministry, and for His Church. I will decree the patterns that He wants to displace the system with. So, I will tear down the work of the enemy, and I will put God in its place.

Then, we will see the Church arise and shine. We will see the kings of this world and the nations drawn to the brightness of that rising. We will see the Church taking the lead, not in arrogance, but in boldness.

And having done all... We will most definitely stand!

CHAPTER 12

Taking the Land — Displacement Warfare

CHAPTER 12 — TAKING THE LAND — DISPLACEMENT WARFARE

I am not a patient person. When I compare the Word of God and the promises of God with my circumstance, I am impatient of the fact that things on this earth are not as they are in heaven.

I am impatient of the fact that God promised me one thing, but it seems that the devil is having a run with another.

> *1 John 5:4-5 For whatever is born of God overcomes the world. And this is the victory that has overcome the world—our faith.*
> *5 Who is he who overcomes the world, but he who believes that Jesus is the Son of God?*

Clearly, God has called us to rule and reign in this life. We are called in the name of Christ Jesus. Those who are in the blood of Christ Jesus are called to overcome, and to rule and reign in this world.

So tell me, why aren't you impatient when you look at the circumstances in your life? It is about time, Church of God, that you become impatient. It is about time that you become discontent with being the servants and the scum when God has called you to be the kings and queens who rule and reign.

Yet, you are groveling under the works of the enemy. You quiver under the enemy's arrows that fly past your

head. You shake in shame and fear. You tremble at the
name of Lucifer. When are we, as a Church, going to be
peculiar as a kingdom to rule and reign? When will we
subdue this earth, as God has promised us?

We have looked at the subject of spiritual warfare. I
have shown you how satan gains license, and how he
has established strongholds in your life. I have taught
you about the systems of this world and the package
that the enemy has perfectly arranged to subdue the
kingdom of God.

HOW TO ESTABLISH GOD'S KINGDOM ON EARTH

Now I ask you, child of God, as you have come to the
fullness of understanding of how satan works, and how
he has established himself in this earth to continue his
reign - what have you done to establish the kingdom of
God in this earth today?

Are you just a pitiful victim of the work of satan? Are
you to remain in this world as weak and foolish, and as
a victim to every little arrow that the enemy throws in
your direction?

As organized as the enemy is, and as much as he has
arrayed his systems perfectly on the battlefield, let's
not forget that we have the power, authority, and all
the weapons of warfare that we need to overcome.

However, I am calling you to do more than just
overcome. Make no mistake - this chapter is not about

overcoming. Please do not misunderstand me. There is no desire in my heart to overcome the enemy.

I do not wish to overcome him because he was already overcome two thousand years ago. If just overcoming is as small as you are thinking, then you have not begun to understand the concept of spiritual warfare.

1. SPIRITUAL WARFARE

What is the purpose of spiritual warfare? Is it to overcome the enemy? No! It is to rule and reign with Christ and to subdue this earth. It is to be a city set upon a hill, to shine to every nation, and to be an example to every tribe and tongue. It is to draw many to Christ.

That is what spiritual warfare is. The purpose of spiritual warfare is not about binding demons, but about establishing Christ in this earth. When you can grasp this concept, you begin to get an inkling of the level of warfare that God is calling us to as a Church.

Certainly, this is the case for those that are called to the fivefold ministry, and this new move that God is releasing into the earth right now.

You are now beginning to just grasp an inkling of what it means to do spiritual warfare.

How much time do you spend binding demons, dealing with curses, speaking forth healing, and running around putting out spiritual fires in your life? In comparison, how much time do you spend establishing the kingdom of God in this earth?

There is a difficult way and an easy way. This chapter is all about the easy way. Every kingdom needs good defenses. Every kingdom should have its watchman on the walls. They should be armed and ready to warn when the enemy is coming.

They should see the cracks in the wall and know where the enemy is getting in. By all means, as I have already taught you, make sure that you have established your castle walls and that you are not giving satan any license in your life.

GAINING THE UPPER HAND ON THE BATTLEFIELD

That is my first point of displacement warfare. Yes, do that spiritual warfare and start gaining an upper hand on the battlefield of your mind. Get an upper hand on all the strongholds of the enemy.

You should be getting to the place where you have silenced the voice of the enemy so much that the voice of God is echoing through your soul. However, you spend so much time fighting spirits of lust, fear, guilt, condemnation, jealousy and pride.

You are continually binding the demons. When are you going to get to the place where you realize that until your mind is renewed, you are not going to hear God coming with a message of faith, hope, and love?

How about a spirit of love and faith for your fear? You are so busy binding this and that demon... why don't you just put something else in its place? Would it not be so much easier if you woke up in the morning harassed with love?

What if you stepped out in the world, and faith overcame you? Is that not the victorious life that God has called us to? How much time have you spent on this battlefield of yours, renewing your mind through the Word?

Have you been putting faith in the promises that God has given you, meditating on them day and night? That is what Joshua did.

God gave him a plan to take the Promised Land, but he did not leave it at that. Even before he put a foot on the land at Canaan, he was renewing his mind and meditating on those promises day and night.

He remained in the presence of God. Even before he headed out, how did he prepare for war? Do you see him there sharpening his sword? No. He was sharpening the sword of his soul. He meditated and meditated until the reality of God's promise was his only reality.

Tell me, child of God, what is your reality today? What is the first thing that comes to your mind about the life that you have and the life that God has promised you? What is the life that you see in your future?

I am not talking about dreams, hopes, and fantasies, but about your reality. What is your reality today?

When you meditate on the promises of God and on His Word, when a demon finds a crack in your wall, it is only too obvious because it is in such stark contrast to what God has been telling you your entire life.

Sounds like a bit of effort, doesn't it?

I taught an entire message on faith, hope, and love, and on how to get this soul of yours into shape. What if we truly got this battlefield of ours in such good shape that the influence of God was stronger on us than the influence of the devil?

THE ENEMY'S TACTICS EXPOSED

I already taught you how satan tries to rattle you on the battlefield. He sends arrows, circumstances, and people your way. What is the purpose of all the warfare and the heaviness that you feel when the arrows are coming at you?

These things are to rattle you and to make you sin. When you have curses in your life and these strongholds in your life, it is as if the thundering sound of that weapon of warfare is so loud that you cannot hear the voice of your Savior.

When you engage in spiritual warfare, you are shutting the devil up, so that you can hear the sweet, tender voice of the Lord Jesus deep inside of you. Yet, what if you took some time to make the voice of the Lord just a little bit louder?

What if the voice of faith and hope were louder? That is true spiritual warfare. That does not just tear down strongholds, but builds a couple of your own.

BUILDING STRONGHOLDS OF FAITH, HOPE AND LOVE

We spoke about the strongholds of the enemy and that he uses, pride, bitterness, and others that he lobs at you all the time to rattle you.

Let's take this a step further. How about we build us a stronghold of faith, hope, and love? We need strongholds in our lives that continue to reproduce themselves as we sleep and walk out our lives.

The enemy spent a lot of time getting you under that bondage of fear, lust, guilt, pride, and every other struggle that is in you. What if you took some time building strongholds of faith, hope, and love?

These would naturally neutralize the strongholds of the enemy. This is displacement warfare. Are you displacing fear with faith in your life? Are you displacing bitterness with love, and pride with hope?

When you displace these things, you do not have to run around binding demons all the time. The devil has to bow to the name of Jesus. He has to succumb to the blood. You know all of this already. You know your authority.

However, there is an easier way. You can establish strongholds in your life that do the warfare for you. You do not have to keep binding demons all the time. Your spirit, soul, and body can be in a place of submission to the spirit of God all the time.

A curse cannot touch you, unless it has a place to land. So, sort yourself. Make sure that it does not have a place to land. This is displacement warfare.

Satan brings sickness to your body, attacks in your finances, family, and those closest to you. There is nothing worse than receiving close attacks that have a way of sneaking their way into making cracks in your wall.

Has it ever occurred to you that those are rebellious circumstances?

EXCUSE ME MR. CIRCUMSTANCE...

> *2 Corinthians 10:5 Casting down arguments and every high thing that exalts itself against the knowledge of God, bringing every thought into captivity to the obedience of Christ*

"Excuse me, Mr. Circumstance. I never gave you permission to stand against me today. Excuse me, you pain in my body, are you seriously in rebellion to the Word of God? Did I not remind you that the blood of Christ was shed and that, by His stripes, I am healed?

Excuse me - I am a little impatient with this attack on my finances. I am impatient with this attack on my family, my marriage, my body, my ministry and my life. Excuse me, circumstances. You are an imagination. I cast you down, and I call you into obedience to the name of the Lord Jesus Christ.

I have had enough of you. You come into line with the Word of God. You, things in earth, come into line with what it is in accordance to heaven."

You see circumstances as a shadow - sand in your hands that you cannot seem to grasp. It just falls through your fingers. You have to run around and try to make a sand castle with it.

The Word of God is quite clear, and the promises that God has given you are quite clear. Anything that is contrary to that is just plain rebellion, which is the sin of witchcraft. I am not doing any witchcraft in my life, so you – circumstance – you can just come in line with the Word of God.

This is displacement. Displacement is not...

"I bind that demon for giving me a flat tire."

"I bind that demon for this and that demon for that."

Why don't you just send forth a decree of so much power that it pushes those demons out of the way? I am talking about the kind of word that God sent forth, where He just sneezed and the entire Red Sea parted.

I do not care how many demons are trying to hold that water together. I do not care how much Pharaoh and all of his troops were behind the Israelites, trying to take them out. The Word of God had enough power to separate those waters, and drown those Egyptians.

When you come with the power of God, it is the ultimate warfare. What I have taught you about breaking links and dealing with open doors stops the enemy from coming back. When satan has license in your life, he is given that license to continue to bear pressure.

BRINGING FORTH CREATION

So, it is essential that you close those doors so that he does not have that license. Why? This way, it is easier for you. Then, when you come with that creative word of authority from the Scriptures and promises that God has given you, creation takes place in your life.

Then, the enemy will not come in to kill, steal, and destroy. Have you had it where your faith has been at a place where you speak forth a word, and you see God move?

Yes, God moves powerfully, and He provides. You get healed, relationships come right, doors open, and ministries flourish. Praise you Jesus. Then suddenly, satan creeps in underneath your foundation and steals, kills, and destroys.

Something goes wrong with your body, something goes wrong with your finances. Why does this happen? You did not seal up the cracks.

You have dealt with every sin in your life, closed every door, and done everything that you know how to do. But, you are not seeing the force of creation in your life. You are not seeing any blessing. Why not?

DOING WARFARE WILL NOT AUTOMATICALLY ENSURE BLESSING

Did you really think that dealing with a demon automatically blesses you from the heavenly realm? Where in the Word does it say, "Bind a demon, and God will bless you?" Think about that. People think that doing spiritual warfare is automatically going to ensure blessing.

That is like saying, "Satan got the key to my house. I discovered it and took the key away."

Is just taking the key away automatically going to return all the furniture that he stole? Is that going to repair the walls that he tore down? For that, you need the power of God. You need to put the Word on your lips and walk on the land.

Joshua could survey the land. He could even walk around the walls of Jericho. He even killed the enemy. Yet, after they killed their enemy, did they possess the Promised Land? No, they just killed the enemy.

You think that if you kill the enemy, you automatically possess the land? No, we need displacement. Once you closed those doors and stopped satan from creeping in, you need to start building and establishing something new.

That is why I took you through all these other steps of closing the doors and giving the Lord license. Yes, you need to call circumstances into line. You need to call those systems into line as well.

SYSTEMS — LAYING A PRAYER FOUNDATION

> **Revelation 11:15** *Then the seventh angel sounded: And there were loud voices in heaven, saying, "The kingdoms of this world have become the kingdoms of our Lord and of His Christ, and He shall reign forever and ever!"*

"The devil is so big."

Why don't you just put Christ in his place in this world? We have been given this world to rule and reign. What we say goes. God said to Adam, "Here is the earth. I have given it to you. Subdue the earth."

Man has set up the enemy's systems and kingdoms. We have the world doing what the devil wants it to do.

"Woe is me. Poor, little Christian. How can I fight against all these political decisions? How can I fight against what my president does, what my community does?"

You can get on your knees and put Jesus at the helm of those systems. You could pray, "I cause this system to be a blessing to the Church."

PUT GOD ON HIS THRONE

If God could call Pharaoh and Nebuchadnezzar His servants, I am sure the president of your country counts too. Even in his sin, God can arrange circumstances to bear blessing on the Church, on your community, on your family, and on your life.

You want to play God and say who is going to be in power.

"This is what I think."

Forget about what you think. Just give God control and let Him figure out the details. He is God. He sees the world as a chessboard. You see your one, little community. You just get God on the throne, and He will tell you what to do from there.

If He needs you to do something, like He did with Mordecai and Esther, you can be sure that He will tap you on the shoulder to let you know.

It would have been foolish for Esther to have gone before the king if she had not first become his wife. She needed to be in position first before she could have an influence. She did not ask for that position or seek out that position.

God said, "I need someone to save my people... ah... there you are!"

Was it because Esther and Mordecai were so righteous? Hardly! It almost happened by accident, didn't it?

She did not wake up one day, praying to be the queen. It was because of the promise that God made to His people, and because of the decrees that the prophets had sent out before their captivity, that caused this series of events to take place. God established His people, His way.

All we need to do is be like those prophets and give God license in this earth. Yet, you are so busy trying to do it by yourself that you have forgotten that the power is on your tongue. It is certainly the role of the prophet to send forth the decrees that will establish the Church in this earth.

Yes, you call those systems into line. "You! Financial system! Excuse me, but the last time I read the Word of God, it said that you will hoard up the silver and the clothing, but the just will put it on.

What is up with this? I am not seeing any clothing and silver being passed on to the righteous. Come in line with the Word of God! This earth belongs to us. In the name of Jesus, you, financial system, will be arranged to speak and become a favorable condition for the Church."

"You, political system, whatever laws are passed, I call you into line right now in the name of Jesus. I call you in line with the Word and the promises of God. Whatever decisions are made, they will be favorable to the Church."

We wrestle not with flesh and blood but with principalities and powers in high places. This kind of warfare does more than bind demons. It gives God control.

THE ULTIMATE POWER

What is the ultimate power? Is it to go around taking out foot soldiers, or is it to have a new king put on the throne who can command the foot soldiers?

What are you doing? You are running around fighting this little demon and that little demon. You are fighting too small. It is time that you go to the top and take on Lucifer himself.

"Oh no! The devil?"

Yes, the devil. He fell from heaven and took a third of the angels. Do the math, people! We just have a little bit of an upper hand here. We are so afraid of the devil and his hordes that we have forgotten what is behind us.

We forget about the blood, and if that is not enough, we even have a couple of legions of angels. We have the King of Kings, the warrior of warriors, Himself.

I do not see the devil separating any Red Seas for Pharaoh and his crowd. Where do you see the devil saving his people so miraculously? You forget how powerful your God is.

You just need to give Him license. Why? We need to do it because He gave this world to us, and it is for us to give it back to Him. We need to be like the twelve elders in Revelation 4:10 who took their crowns and said, "Here, you are the one that is worthy. Take my authority."

WHERE IS YOUR CROWN?

What does a crown speak of? It speaks of authority, right? This is a beautiful display of putting God on the throne. It says that the twelve elders came, took off their crowns, and laid them at the feet of the Lord.

Where is your crown today? When you take your authority as man, the authority that God has given you, and you give it over to Him, you give Him a place to rule and reign in this earth.

This is Christ being put on the throne of your body, your life, your circumstances, and the systems of this world. That is just step one. That is just spiritual warfare, pure and simple.

There is a step two...

2. Building New Systems

Step two and three are probably the most untaught, but the most powerful, weapons of warfare that we have available to us in the Church.

As God is resurrecting the apostolic ministry and birthing a new movement in this world, He is engaging satan at a level of warfare that he has not seen since the day of Adam and Eve.

The Movement

There is a creation taking place that displaces the theft and destruction that he has brought about in this earth. Do you want to know the best way to displace satan in your life and in this world?

Start a movement!

You get so busy, scrambling around and trying to take this land that God has given you. Tell me, child of God, once you have the land, what are you doing with it?

"I have a land. Check out my land. It is a big land. It is valuable land."

"What are you doing with your land?"

"I am defending it. It is my land."

Why did the ancients go into so much effort to gain land? Let me give you a little bit of a history lesson. They needed to survive. More land meant more crops.

This meant resources and more places that they could build stuff on.

We are so busy trying to claim our land.

"This is my land, devil. This is my land."

The devil is like, "I know it is your land." He waits for a crack, and then, "Hey, I have some of your land."

"Give me my land back."

"I have some of your land."

"Give me my land back."

For goodness sakes, this is exhausting! You have to go to the next level. You cannot carry on like this for another couple of thousand years. When the children of Israel took the Promised Land by sword, they did not do a victory dance and then just camp out.

TIME TO GET PRACTICAL

They built big cities. The Word does not call us a piece of land on top of a hill. It calls us a city that is set on a hill. How difficult is it to take a land back when it has a city upon it with city walls?

How hard is it to take a land when it has weapons of warfare, watchmen, and towers? It is very hard. Yet, you are so busy trying to defend your land that you have not taken time to build anything on it. That is why starting a movement, establishing something new, like Ezra did, is vital.

> ***Ezra 3:10-11*** *When the builders laid the foundation of the temple of the Lord, the priests stood in their apparel with trumpets, and the Levites, the sons of Asaph, with cymbals, to praise the Lord, according to the ordinance of David king of Israel.*
>
> *11 And they sang responsively, praising and giving thanks to the Lord: "For He is good, for His mercy endures forever toward Israel." Then all the people shouted with a great shout, when they praised the Lord, because the foundation of the house of the Lord was laid.*

It was only when they rebuilt that city that it became their own. When do you know that the land that God has promised you is truly yours? It is when you begin to build on it.

You talk about all the things that God wants to do in your life. You do all the spiritual warfare, thinking that if you just bind a demon and lay the groundwork in prayer that this will automatically establish your ministry.

Can we just be very practical here? There comes a time when you have to get a bank account. There comes a time when you actually have to start your ministry. You have to do something with the land that God has given to you.

We need to start a movement in the Church. We need to begin doing something with the message that God has given to us. We need to build. There is no use doing warfare and nothing else.

It is no use just having a good idea or just having a vision, a hope, and a prayer. You have to begin to establish something. We need to begin building this new movement and putting our hands in the soil, not just complaining about the Church and what it doesn't have.

ESTABLISH YOUR MINISTRY

What are you doing about it? Are you going from church to church and complaining? That is not establishing anything. You need to establish your ministry. I love what it says in 2 Samuel 5.

He speaks about what became of his city, the city of David. However, he had to overcome it first. So, he went in and found those cracks in the wall. He took that city down, and he took that land.

> *2 Samuel 5:9-10 Then David dwelt in the stronghold, and called it the City of David. And David built all around from the Millo and inward.*
> *10 So David went on and became great, and the Lord God of hosts was with him.*

He did not just take the city. He built the city. He established the city. Once you have done your spiritual warfare, there has to come a time when you take action. You need to set up a structure and organize.

This is where a lot of the great evangelists failed. They did part one, beautifully. They were strong in spiritual warfare. Demons manifested - they cast them out. They got many saved, and they did a fantastic job.

However, they never left a structure behind to continue the work that they had started. What happens with every great evangelist? They fizzle out along with their anointing. Then, as the anointing leaves, so does his entire ministry.

That is why I said that a movement is the best way to do spiritual warfare. This breaks people past their mindsets and gives them something new.

Until you build, structure, and organize your ministry, and get it built on a solid foundation, the land does not belong to you. Until the temple and the walls had been built, it was just a hope and a prayer.

Once you have gained the land, and God has opened the doors, what are you doing with it? Here is the little catch to our plan. You and I are not the only ones who have authority in this earth. Every man does, whether saved or unsaved.

We are human beings, and we all have authority. You should know from your own experience that your own fears and sin have allowed satan license in your life and have conditioned the way that you think.

This has conditioned the way that you walk this life out. You know your own journey, and you know how hard this has been for you to break free of thinking, "I cannot do this" and then get to the place of thinking, "I can do all things through Christ."

You know how hard this has been, right? Do not forget though, that you are not the only person in this world.

If we want to see a movement, build a ministry, or something that remains in this world, it is going to take other people. Herein lies the secret of displacement.

3. DISPLACEMENT WARFARE IN THE HEARTS OF MAN

If you want to displace satan in this world, you start by displacing him in the hearts and minds of God's people.

> **Romans 12:2-4** *And do not be conformed to this world, but be transformed by the renewing of your mind, that you may prove what is that good and acceptable and perfect will of God.*
> *3 For I say, through the grace given to me, to everyone who is among you, not to think of himself more highly than he ought to think, but to think soberly, as God has dealt to each one a measure of faith.*
> *4 For as we have many members in one body, but all the members do not have the same function*

He starts out by saying, "Stop it with this worldly thinking. Deal with it. You are not thinking right. You are thinking according to the patterns of this world."

However, he does not just leave it there. He goes on to tell them about renewing their minds.

He says, "Let's put a new picture in your mind. You are thinking along the course of the world. You are members of the same body. Each one has a place. This is where we all belong, and this is how we all fit in."

What did Paul do right there? He displaced the devil in their heads. He took out worldly thinking, and he displaced it with godly thinking.

Think about this for a minute. When we displace victim mentality or poverty mentality, we displace the demonic influence that satan has on God's people. What kind of warfare is that?

You know that a lot of the warfare that you are experiencing in your life is through circumstances and other people. You do have your own stuff to deal with, which we covered in a lot of detail earlier. However, a lot of it comes from others.

So, how are we going to change the world? One person at a time. If they can change the way that they think, they will not give satan license, which means that there will be less for the devil to keep piggy backing on in the Church.

We need to stop trying to tell people what is wrong, and create a movement that helps them to think differently.

So tell me, when you get opposition, how does that make you feel?

I love it when someone comes knocking at my door and says, "You are wrong!"

I just love that. Please, come and tell me what an idiot I am. It makes my day. I respond right away with, "Really? You are right. I have been wrong my whole life. I am going to stop what I am doing and just listen to you."

Perhaps a tad sarcastic, but certainly quite true! No one in this world loves rejection and opposition!

However, do you know how much we do that to each other?

"Your doctrine is wrong."

"You dress incorrectly."

"You are failing God."

"You should run your ministry this way… "

THERE HAS TO BE MORE...

That is not what I am talking about when I say, "renew their minds." I am talking about starting a movement and showing people a different way.

We were just talking amongst the team recently on the subject of the reformation and Martin Luther, and how the people had been bound by the doctrine of the Catholic Church. In those days, they did not even have the Bible for the common man to read.

Not even all the priests had the Bible to read. If they wanted to read it, they had to go to where the texts were. Keep in mind - we did not have printing presses just yet.

God started a reformation, a revolution in the Church, through Martin Luther. He woke up one day, thinking, "There has to be more to God than what I am seeing here." God put a fire in his heart.

The printing press was invented, and the reformation started to gain momentum. For the first time, Christians started to see the light. Luther did not need to run around telling Christians that they were believing something wrong.

He just had to show them grace. They were so hungry and thirsty for grace that they were quite ready to let go of the dirty, moldy, stale bread that they thought would feed them.

It is about time that the fivefold ministry rose up and gave a message of faith, hope, and love. It is time that they start painting a picture of that city on a hill that God has called us to be, instead of walking around telling everybody that they are wrong.

We need to change the hearts and minds of God's people. When we do that, satan does not have license anymore. When the Church believes that God is punishing them all the time, satan has a heyday.

He can do whatever he wants in the name of God, and people will believe it. He has a flourishing tree in which he can roost. However, what if we taught God's people that God has set them free, and He whom the Son sets free is free indeed?

"He has not called you to suffer or to be in bondage. He has called us to rule and reign." That doctrine automatically deals with the demon.

Are you beginning to grasp the logic that I am trying to impart to you here?

Breaking Faith in Satan

Is it important to deal with demons? Yes, but that is the quick and easy part. This should not be the bulk of your warfare. Your warfare is found each time that you stand behind the pulpit, read the Word, or give a prophetic word.

That is warfare. Why? It is because this is how you are displacing what people believe to be true. Satan has roosted in the faith given to him. He is puffed up with pride, through the messages that give him so much power in our lives.

When are we going to rise up and pull the rug out from under him? We have Christians giving him so much license through ill-placed faith.

"I believe this is God making me suffer."

The devil is laughing and having fun with this. He has us fighting so much amongst ourselves all "in the name of God." He is laughing all the way to the bank.

You have to change the way that God's people think. When you do that, you do not have to bind that demon. When someone stops believing in demons, you do not need to bind them. You do not need to take authority over them anymore because they have no place to rest anymore.

That is why doctrine is probably one of the biggest strongholds in your life, for both good and evil. It can keep you in bondage to satan, or it can keep you under the blood and faith in Christ.

WARFARE THROUGH SPIRITUAL PARENTING

CHAPTER 13 – WARFARE THROUGH SPIRITUAL PARENTING

You have been shaped and influenced through the templates, experiences, and doctrines throughout your life. You have a foundation of disappointments, hurts of the past, and demonic influences you received through impartations. Add to that, doctrine taught through parents and generational curses, and it does not take much to see how much we have been conditioned for failure or success.

Our souls have been conditioned so much by the spirit of the world. We have Paul saying, "You are not of the world, so stop acting like it."

I do not know about you, but I have often found myself striving against that spirit of the world. It is as if everything in my flesh is craving that spirit of the world. Yet, knowing the Word of God, I know that I should not be wanting those things.

O WRETCHED MAN…

I know that I should not feel prideful or even hunger after worldly things. I know that I should not get angry. However, everything in my flesh seems to follow after the systems of the world. Of course, once you do that, satan just jumps on board.

How do you deal with that? How do you overcome all those impartations and programming in your mind, year after year?

You get rid of it through two processes - spiritual parenting and discipleship. How did you get that way? How did you get to the point of believing that satan has the upper hand? How did you get to the point of believing that bad things always happen to you and that you just have to accept it?

"God is never going to heal you."

"You are never going to rise up in your ministry."

"You are never going to succeed. You are just a failure, a sinner, and a loser."

How are you going to take these voices out of your head and throw them away? You need to be reprogrammed. Is that not what Paul was saying about the renewing of your mind?

Through the Word and through doctrine, you can renew your mind. When your mind is renewed, satan does not have a place to land anymore. That is why God is raising up leaders in today's day and age to re-parent and change the way that people think.

FAMILY GENERATIONAL CURSES

It is that generational thinking, from family to family, that keeps the curses of your family in place. I mentioned how generational curses are established through repeated, un-repented sin.

You, as a child, are brought up in that family. Every mindset that you were taught, every programming that you were given, predisposes you to the kind of thinking that accepts that sin as the norm.

Even though you always have had a choice to whether you are going to make that sin your own or not, because of the way that you were brought up and what you were taught to be true, it is so hard to make the right decision.

The minute that you make that sin your own, you get the whole package with it. You get the generational curses of sickness, poverty, destruction, and theft. Everyone has their own, right?

There is an easier way. Why don't you just get a new bloodline through re-parenting? We need to have a few more Moses', Pauls' and Peters' in our midst in the Church. Moses went so far that he even renamed Joshua.

How about that? They took on sons, gave them a new bloodline, and a new way of thinking. With that new way of thinking, blessing came. It predisposed them to make the right decision. It displaced the old with the new.

ARCHETYPE

I had read a good book a while back. It is not even a Christian book, but a worldly one. It is called *Rich Dad, Poor Dad*. If you have ever been in any of those self-help teachings, I am sure that you know what I am talking about.

In this book, this guy shares how his rich dad, who was not his real dad, took him on and taught him how to be rich and successful. He saw how his rich dad thought and how his poor dad thought. It was really like him having a spiritual father.

Naturally, he displaced all his poor dad's thinking mentalities with his rich dad's thinking mentalities, and he ended up becoming rich.

How did this happen? It was because he changed his mindset. That is what spiritual parenting does - it changes the way that you think. Then, once it has changed the way that you think, you are predisposed to the same blessing that the spiritual parent has.

They have that blessing because they believe it to be true. Without faith, it is impossible to please God. Sometimes, our doubts overwhelm our mustard seed of faith.

When someone believes something so strongly to be true, that faith triggers the success and blessing in their lives.

The reason why you find it so hard to walk in success and blessing is because everything in your heart and mind is saying, "I cannot do it. I will never succeed. I was born to be, and always will be, a failure. This is my lot in life. This is the way it was for my father, his father, and his father, and it is the same for me."

SPIRITUAL DNA

It is time to break the line of failure!

Until there are men and women of faith who will make themselves accountable, and rise up to have their bad generational curses, thinking, and archetype smashed and renewed in the presence of the Father, then we are not going to see change in the Church.

You learn about Christ on the knee of your mother, and through the words of your father. Whether those words are, "He exists" or "He does not exist," that is what is established in you. Faith, or the lack of it, is borne in the heart of a child.

What were you programmed to believe your whole life?

Now, you feel the power of God inside of you, in your spirit. You feel birthing, passion, vision, hope and a future. Everything in your body and your mind seems to press against the truth, and you are in travail. You are as a woman in childbirth trying so hard to release this baby, but everything is holding it back.

Is it the spirit of God that is wrong? Is it the hand of God that is weak that it cannot redeem or save you?

No! You do not believe that it will save you. Your fear is greater than your faith.

We can go back to step one and renew our minds in the Word again and again. You can do it! Many have done it and overcome with faith, testimony, and the Blood. However, there is an easier way.

This is what God is doing in the Church today. This is why He is raising up apostolic fathers and mothers - spiritual parents, who will change the way that people think. They will impart to them a new spiritual DNA.

They will impart a DNA of faith, hope, and love - A DNA of possibility. They will say, "You will overcome in the name of Jesus! You better believe that you are called to rule and reign. You can do anything that God has called you to do. You are made in the image of Christ. You are above and not beneath. You are the head and not the tail."

Do you want to know why the Jews were so rich all the time and why they succeeded? It is because they believed. From generation to generation, it was taught to them.

"You are a peculiar nation. You are better than everyone else around you."

Does it seem like, even today, that Jewish people walk around with an air of superiority?

PASS ON A SOLID FOUNDATION

Absolutely! And why not? It is because that is what they have been taught. What are you teaching your children? What have you been taught? What are you teaching the next generation in the Church?

It is only through this parenting that you are going to see a new faith mindset being borne. Who is prepared to be accountable? There is a price to pay to be in this place.

Don't you think that it cost Paul everything? It cost Moses to be at such a level of accountability. So much so that just one mistake, and he was not allowed to see the Promised Land.

ABRAHAM AND SARAH — A NEW GENERATION OF SPIRITUAL PARENTS

There are those that God is raising up in this day and age. The Lord is raising up Abrahams that have been called out of their country, archetype, and everything that they know so that they can establish a new family.

Why did Abraham have to be called out? It is because he could not afford for him to think like the people from which he came. He needed to have a thinking that made the impossible possible.

Could it be possible that God could reach down and touch a man?

Could it be that there was a God of mercy out there, somewhere in the stars, who would enter into a covenant with a man?

In his day and age, this was unfathomable. Yet, it was possible for him because God drew him out of what he knew and where that doctrine was taught, so that he could teach him a new thing.

God did not educate the children of Israel in Egypt. He took them out of Egypt to Mount Sinai, and then revealed His will to them there. God wants to take the Church out of the desert, but let us first get the desert out of the Church.

The desert is in our hearts, minds, preconceived ideas, and in our archetypes.

TAKING THE WORLD OUT OF THE CHURCH

Where does satan have license? This is a teaching on spiritual warfare, so why am I talking about re-parenting?

It is simple. Satan has control over the systems of the world. He has control over the archetypes and makes sure that everybody is doing everything the way that he wants them to do it. So, if you want to displace him, then you need to displace the world in the Church.

Do that and... what do you know? The devil is gone.

Is that not what the Scriptures say? You are in the world, but not of it. If you want to get rid of the devil in the Church, then get rid of the world in the Church. He is controlling the world. So, if you get rid of the world, the devil is gone.

You are so busy binding the devil, however, the world is in the Church, so the devil keeps getting in through the back door.

The prophets are binding the devil in every single meeting, and for a few minutes, the devil is gone. The Blood is on the floor, and he cannot come in. Then, everyone leaves, and the devil is back again for the next meeting.

It is exhausting. Get the systems in line. Get the world out of the Church. Get the wrong doctrine out of the Church. Get the heresy out of the Church, and then the demon has nothing to have a party in.

You will then have liberty in the spirit. That is displacement warfare. Now this is not a call for everyone in the body of Christ. I hope you are grasping that concept by now.

I am not going to give this message to a new convert, and say, "Please go and establish a foundation to displace the enemy in the church."

FIVEFOLD MINISTERS COME FORTH

I am calling forth the apostles and the rest of the fivefold ministry to do their job.

Teachers, where are you? Why are you not displacing that doctrine in the minds of God's people? Why are you not giving a doctrine of faith, hope and love, of possibility, of success, and a mentality of passion and expectation for what God wants to do?

Prophets, where are you? Are you teaching the Church what the voice of their Savior looks like, sounds like, and feels like, so that when the spirit of the world comes into the church, they recognize it for what it is?

Pastors, where are you laying down the law, and establishing the Word of God into the hearts of the Church - just like a mother would with a child day by day? Are you shaping the way that they think and feel - giving them guidelines for conduct to live by?

Evangelists, where are you with your fire? Are you exposing the work of the devil so that the people can see the idols that they are worshipping, and have their eyes and ears opened?

Apostles, where are you with your mandate to lay a new foundation?

If you want to displace the devil and overcome his works in the Church, then it is time to build. It is only when you begin to build that you have not just taken back your land, but you start encroaching on some of the enemy's territory too.

ESTABLISHING THE LAND

CHAPTER 14 – ESTABLISHING THE LAND

I am not satisfied to just take my land. This whole world is my land. I am not happy to have just my little ministry, my little building, my little team, and my little happiness where everyone is content.

That is like the New Testament church in Jerusalem, a little happy club. Jesus said to them, "Go forth into all the world."

It is time that we go forth into all the world. Once you have established your "happy club," you should be using it as a base from which to send out some sneak attacks into the enemy's camp.

He has been traipsing over your battlefield, into your mind, and finding the cracks in the walls in your city. He has established weapons of warfare on your land to take you out with. He has done it with fear, guilt, pride, and bitterness.

He has been taking us out one at a time. We are dismantling those weapons and strongholds, but that is not good enough. It is not good enough to keep the devil at bay.

When all is said and done, it is time that the fivefold ministry straps on the shield of faith, puts a sword in their hand, puts on a helmet of salvation, and goes to make a few cracks in the enemy's wall.

You have been defending, but it is time that you go, as Joshua did, and walk around those walls of Jericho until they come down. Then, you cannot stop at the walls of Jericho, but you must go into the city to destroy and tear down every last work that was built there.

We will not stop after we have taken the city, but we will go forth into the land. With every enemy, stronghold, city and system - whether of education, politics, commercial, financial, or medical - we will go into every last one of the enemy's cities and tear them down brick by brick.

We will establish it again and put our King of Kings on the throne. That is warfare. I want to own it and give it to Christ for His glory. That is what God has called us to do as a Church. We are a little bit behind schedule.

WATCH OUT FOR THESE PITFALLS

1. DOING WARFARE WITHOUT BUILDING

You are making some mistakes though. You are doing warfare without taking time to build. You deal with your sin, pull down the stronghold, and tell the systems to come into line. That is great. It is great that Joshua walked around the walls of Jericho.

However, he did not stop there. David did not stop after he took Jerusalem either. He built it into a city, and then it was called, "The City of David." It was not called "The City of David" while it was still sitting in ruins.

At that time, it was just the land of David... the ruins of David. It was "The City of David" after he established it into one.

How did Solomon take the land even more than his father? It said that, in the days of Solomon, bronze was considered worthless, and silver was like dust. There was gold here, there, and everywhere.

He was the king. He did not pick up a sword. Do you know how he took the land? He built the land. Solomon built city after city.

He built his house and the temple. He was a builder. It was in the building of the cities that he established Israel as a success. They got to see the fruit of what God promised David.

Is the warfare necessary?

Yes, David had to pick up his sword. He had to overcome the land. Yet, until the land had been built, the children of Israel did not know prosperity.

David taking the land stopped the oppression, but it did not make them wealthy. It took Solomon to make them wealthy. If you are just taking the land and taking the land, then you are going to have a big land of ruins.

Great, you can boast about your land. But, you are not going to change the Church until you start building the ministries, getting your feet on the ground, starting this movement and being loud, proud, and confident enough to do it now.

We cannot sit around saying, "I am waiting on the Lord. In the meantime, I am just going to bind some more demons."

2. BUILDING WITHOUT DOING WARFARE

On the other hand, we have people out there doing so much for God and starting church after church, but they never take time to do spiritual warfare. Then they think, "What happened? Why did the devil take me out?"

Did you seal up the cracks in your wall first? Did you make sure that you had watchmen on your walls?

Before you leave your city and you go and attack another city, you need to make sure that your city at home is defended. You have to make sure that you have walls around your city, and there are no big strongholds of the enemy in your field around your city.

Then, when you go out to do warfare and build, you know that everyone at home is doing ok.

However, we have people going out saying, "I built this and that ministry. I started this and that work."

Then, they cannot understand why each and every work is taken out from under them. If you want to do effective warfare and displace the work of satan in the

Church, you are going to need to do effective warfare, build, and displace.

3. DISPLACEMENT WITHOUT BUILDING

You even have those, (this is where I made my mistake), who go around displacing everything in the hearts of God's people but do not give them a place to actually walk it out.

So, you spend years changing the mindsets, helping them overcome, getting them to flow in the gifts of the Spirit, and getting them all fired up. Then, they have no church, ministry, or anywhere to go to actually shine with the light that you have imparted to them.

You did not take time to establish your ministry. You do not have a structure. You do not have an organization or anywhere to send them after you have done all this work for them.

You just go around setting people free, and then you have nowhere to send them after they are free. So, what do they do? Like a dog that returns to its vomit, they go back to their bondage. Why? It is because that is the only place that they have to walk out the little bit that they have.

What is the point of spending so much time with people and teaching them prosperity and other things, and then you do not give them a place to walk that out? You are not giving them an opportunity or an avenue in which to flow in those gifts.

"I am sure that something will come up. God will open the door."

I hated it actually. I liked the parenting part, working with people, firing them up and getting them excited about what God is doing in the Church.

They would leave, go into the status quo church, get crushed, and come crawling back all sad and pitiful. I would have to patch them up and send them out again.

The Lord said to me, "Colette, I know that you are a prophet, but you need to learn a word that you have never applied in your life before. This word is – structure... closely followed by organization."

BUILDING A HEARTH FOR THE FIRE

For some of you, that might be natural, but it was not for me. The Lord had me spend nearly a year structuring my ministry. I nearly died. I wanted to just spill passion everywhere. I wanted to release anointing, fire, and power.

"With just a little bit of fire, we can change the world!"

Then, they needed to come back home to get fired up again because the world was dark, and the winds were strong. The rains came flooding down upon them, and they needed to come back to the fireplace to get comforted and warmed up again.

The Lord had me just work on organization. I was doing all the boring stuff, like opening bank accounts, learning accounting, establishing centers, buying equipment, and figuring out how to live stream.

It was very un-anointed, boring, non-spiritual stuff. However, when I set that structure up, there was a fireplace in which that fire could burn.

What use is a fire unless it is contained and used for something beneficial? We have a wildfire that is going off into the fields and just causing destruction a lot of the time. It is just going out there and burning down houses.

What use is a fire unless it is contained and used for the purpose for which it was lit? There is no use going out and lighting people and setting them on fire if you do not have a place to put them afterwards.

The Lord had me to find a place for each one on my team - a place where they could flourish in both the spiritual and the natural.

Then, when they were discouraged or unsure, and the enemy came at them like a flood, they had a place to retreat to get fired up again. They always had something to go on.

THREE STEPS FOR DISPLACEMENT WARFARE

1. **Spiritual Warfare**

2. **Building of Systems**

3. Changing of Hearts

We need all three. If you are going to displace the enemy, you are going to need to do the spiritual warfare. You are going to need to start building systems - the Church needs systems of its own that will bring a godly influence on His people.

We are also going to need to take time to change the hearts of God's people, one at a time, displacing the bondages in their lives. You will learn, the more you read our teachings, that I am not big on what is typically known as "deliverance ministry."

I have come to realize that I do not need to run around casting demons out of people. The Lord has brought us some disciples and spiritual children that have had their fair share of possessing demons, but I never cast a single one out.

I did it the easy way. I just displaced them. I took away the doctrines in their mind that gave it a house to stay in. I cleaned that house out and put something else in its place. I pushed that devil right out and replaced it with the Holy Spirit, the Word of God, and the blood of Christ.

There was nothing else for the demon to hang on to, so it left.

When that demon was manifesting, they could say for themselves, "Do I choose this or that? Do I choose the influence that this demon has had on my life or this promise of success that God has given me? Which am I going to take hold of?"

When I taught them, according to the Word of God, the choice was pretty easy. I did not have to keep casting demons out of them. We should not have to do that. We are renewed in Christ.

I will deal with the manifestation of demons. There is a time and a place for it. I will deal with it in another place, but I am saying, "Do not get so hung up on everything that is wrong."

SHOW ME YOUR CITY!

There is an easier way. Displacement warfare is the easier way. It is the warfare that God is calling us to, as a Church. This is not just my ministry or solely my apostolic mandate. God is calling us to take out the enemy in a new way as a Church.

Why is this? It is because, if the old way worked, the devil would be dead by now. It did not work. It is only keeping the enemy at bay for little moments of time.

We have to do more than just go and pray in a region and bind the princes of the air.

Jolly good for you. You walked around the walls of Jericho. Show me your city! What have you built from that victory?

You just leave that region, and then you go and take down another Jericho. Then, the region that you just prayed at has another wall of Jericho now. You never left anything in its place - what did you expect?

Do you think that the devil is sleeping? Do you think that he is that stupid? He is more organized than you are.

Unless you build something that will continue to displace him, all you have done is rattle his cage a bit. You set the minds of God's people just free enough so that they can grab hold of some truth.

However, you and I both know that it takes more than just one moment of truth to change the way that you think and believe.

You have an experience with Christ, but then you have to walk it out, in fear and trembling. What did you leave behind for them to walk out?

Did you bind that demon so that they can think?

Praise you, Lord! You accomplished step one.

Yet, did you continue to renew their mind in step two? Did you continue to parent them and help them in step three? Did you build something - a ministry that continues to feed them and help them, or are you off to bind the next prince of some other air?

"Let's go bind the prince of America. Then, we can go pray against the prince of Canada."

Could you imagine if Joshua went out, took the land, and never distributed it? They were meant to possess the land, to subdue it, and take ownership of it.

A couple of pennies are falling into place for you, aren't they? You are beginning to understand why you have been under the pressure that you have been, and why the Holy Spirit is leading you in the way that He has.

You are also seeing why it is not good enough to stay on the level that you are at. If God has called you to one of the fivefold ministry as part of this new move, then you have some work to do.

So, let us be like Ezra and Nehemiah. Let us put a sword in one hand and pick up the trowel in the other. Let us do the warfare at the highest level. Then let us build and leave something that remains for the generations to follow!

ABOUT THE AUTHOR

Colette Toach
APOSTOLIC MOVEMENT INTERNATIONAL

Born in Bulawayo, Zimbabwe and raised in South Africa, Colette had a zeal to serve the Lord from a young age. Coming from a long line of Christian leaders and having grown up as a pastor's kid, she is no stranger to the realities of ministry. Despite having to endure many hardships such as her parent's divorce, rejection, and poverty, she continues to follow after the Lord passionately. Overcoming these obstacles early in her life has built a foundation of compassion and desire to help others gain victory in their lives.

Since then, the Lord has led Colette, with her husband, Craig Toach, to establish *Apostolic Movement International,* a ministry to train and minister to Christian leaders all over the world, where they share all the wisdom that the Lord has given them through each and every time they chose to walk through the refining fire in their personal lives, as well as in ministry.

In addition, Colette is a fantastic cook, an amazing mom to not only her 4 natural children, but to her numerous spiritual children all over the world. Colette is also a renowned author, mentor, trainer and a woman that has great taste in shoes! The scripture to "be all things to all men" definitely applies here, and the Lord keeps adding to that list of things each and every day.

How does she do it all? Experience through every book and teaching the life of an apostle firsthand, and get the insight into how the call of God can make every aspect of your life an incredible adventure.

Read more at www.colette-toach.com

Connect with Colette Toach on Facebook!
www.facebook.com/ColetteToach

Check Colette out on Amazon.com at:
www.amazon.com/author/colettetoach

RECOMMENDATIONS BY THE AUTHOR

Note: All reference of AMI refers to Apostolic Movement International.

If you enjoyed this book, I know you will also love the following books and recommendations.

PROPHETIC WARRIOR

Book 5 of the Prophetic Field Guide Series

By Colette Toach

A true warrior holds no excuses of why he cannot defeat his enemy and so is true with a genuine prophet of God. He is ready to take up the weapons of warfare that God has prepared for Him and to set the captive free and to heal the broken hearted.

The prophet that God has called is ready to step onto the battlefield, gain victory in their own lives, and then share the secrets to obtaining victory to all those around them.

Prophet of God, now is the time to face your own limitations and your own bondages and to see what has been holding you back from walking as the warrior that God has called you to be.

Once this is done, you may then step out, pick up your sword and break the chains of wickedness from God's people and the fire in you will blaze as never before.

PROPHETIC COUNTER INSURGENCE

Book 6 of the Prophetic Field Guide Series

By Colette Toach

Learn all about the "prophetic super spy", discover strategies that can be used in spiritual warfare, receive stealth training, find the secrets to dealing with fear of the mind, and where spiritual warfare begins and ends.

It is time to become an agent of Christ, capable of striking down the enemy at any time, in any place, and wherever the Lord calls for it. It is time to take the crippling blows of the enemy and turn them into deathly blows of destruction.

THE MINISTER'S HANDBOOK

By Colette Toach

This is your manual on effective ministry. Whether you are dealing with an unexpected demon manifestation or you need to give marital counsel, you will find the answers here.

Colette Toach gives it to you in plain language. She gives you the steps 1, 2, 3 of how to do what God has called you to do. Keep a copy on hand, because you will come back to it time and time again!

PASTOR TEACHER SCHOOL

www.pastorteacherschool.com

 The Lord had not called me to simply educate. He called me to train. To shape and equip His mighty warriors. I was not allowed any shortcuts. So my training never ended. To this day, He continues to shape and change me. With each lesson I learn, I pass it on to those He sends me.

This is the core of what you will find in the Pastor Teacher School - **Education by means of training**. An interactive experience that causes you to live and walk out the call that God has given to you.

Every lesson is practical, direct, and it... equips! Along with the knowledge, you gain experience and the steps to fulfilling your ministry right now.

There are many who are willing to sell you a book in the Church today, but not many who are willing to *train* you. This is what burns in us and if the Lord has sent you to our ministry, then that is what you can expect from us. A no-nonsense boot camp that is designed to train you for your calling.

You bring your passion for God to the table and we will bring the anointing and skill to train you into what God has intended. **Together... we will change the world!**

- Colette Toach

CONTACT INFORMATION

To check out our wide selection of materials, go to:
www.ami-bookshop.com

Do you have any questions about any products?

Contact us at: +1 (760) 466 - 7679
(9am to 5pm California Time, Weekdays Only)

E-mail Address: admin@ami-bookshop.com

Postal Address:

> A.M.I.
> 5663 Balboa Ave #416
> San Diego, CA 92111, USA

Facebook Page:
http://www.facebook.com/ApostolicMovementInternational

YouTube Page:
https://www.youtube.com/c/ApostolicMovementInternational

Twitter Page: https://twitter.com/apmoveint

Amazon.com Page: www.amazon.com/author/colettetoach

AMI Bookshop – It's not Just Knowledge, It's **Living Knowledge**

Made in the USA
Coppell, TX
24 May 2023

17263726R00134